CHRISTIAN FAITH
AND
CRIMINAL JUSTICE

CHRISTIAN FAITH
AND
CRIMINAL JUSTICE

Toward a Christian Response to Crime and Punishment

by
Gerald Austin McHugh

PAULIST PRESS
New York/Ramsey/Toronto

Library of Congress
Catalog Card Number: 78-58956

ISBN: 0-8091-2105-0

Published by Paulist Press
Editorial Office: 1865 Broadway, New York, N.Y. 10023
Business Office: 545 Island Road, Ramsey, N.J. 07446

Printed and bound in the
United States of America

CONTENTS

Preface   ix

Introduction: Motive & Method   1

1. Christianity and the Evolution
   of Criminal Law and Penology   11

2. Penal Models in the American
   Experience   32

3. Prisoners as People   68

4. Penal Ideology vs. Christian Belief   86

5. The Failure of Christian Witness   130

6. The Foundations of a Christian
   Approach to Criminal Justice   145

7. Human Freedom & Sin   166

8. The Christian Witness Reconsidered:
   "To Prisoners . . . Freedom"   184

9. Faith in Action   200

Notes   212

Bibliography   232

v

To my parents,
Gerald and Louise
whose example and sacrifice
equipped me to write

Every prison that men build is built with bricks of shame/and bound with bars lest Christ should see how men their brothers maim.

> Oscar Wilde
> "The Ballad of Reading Jail"

You may snarl them into sin, and tread them down to hell, but you must love them into repentance, and support them up the ascent to heaven.

> John Reynolds
> Recollections of Windsor Prison

I urge you to keep your Bibles, tracts, medals and organ music. Instead, give us yourselves, your time and help just as He gave of Himself to the sick and the poor and needy. Come out from behind your cloaks of hypocritical self-righteousness and wallow a while with us thieves, pimps, drug addicts and murderers.

If . . . our Christian brothers continue keeping themselves aloof from the men in prison, then let me be the first to proclaim that GOD IS DEAD!

> A. Puchalski
> ". . . and the criminals with him"

PREFACE

As with any project this size, there are many debts to acknowledge, but so few can be acknowledged publicly. I am indebted to my colleagues in the Philadelphia Prisons Thresholds Program, including Jeff Goldstein, Jerry Caughlan, Beth Cooper, Mel & Peg Benson, Craig and Madge Eiser for inspiration and support. A special debt is owed to Sandy and Barbara Bump, who helped me in many ways from beginning to end.

Jean Fix and Brother Joseph Schmidt of the Phila. Archdiocesan Conference on Youth supported this work at its inception and kept it alive. Mrs. Dolores McCaughn of the St. Joseph's College Library provided invaluable resources. Mary McAvinue provided last-minute tactical support.

Rev. Vincent Genovesi supplied critical commentary on aspects of the research, and Rev. Thomas Gleeson S.J. was there to give critical support at numerous junctures. John Haughey, S.J., was an adviser to me throughout.

The College Scholar Program at St. Joseph's College provided the opportunity to conduct the research, and the Jesuit Council for Theological Reflection provided financial resources without which the project would never have been completed.

Mike Alfonsi and Elaine Fitzpatrick gave friendship and helped me keep perspective on the issues.

Sr. Catherine Ellen Kearney was an example of Christian faith in action during the time this book was being revised.

Dr. Thomas McFadden, St. Joseph's College, taught me most of the theology I know, and stood by me as I struggled to write this book. Rev. Ed Denion, S.J., was a constant friend, who never lost faith in the book or my ability to complete it, and his steadfast support made the vision of this book a reality.

My wife Maureen Tate worked with me in the researching and writing of this book, and her love made it possible to continue working when the work seemed too much.

Finally, my parents, to whom this book is dedicated, gave me both the inspiration and the support which made the work possible in the first place.

INTRODUCTION: MOTIVE & METHOD

The Need for Christian Reflection on
Criminal Justice and Penology

Why should the problems of crime and punishment be chosen as a particular focus for Christian reflection? Or, what reason is there for developing a special "theology of criminal justice"?

There are several major justifications for undertaking research of this kind. A key argument is that Christians have a special obligation to confront contemporary penal practices, because historically Christianity has greatly contributed to their evolution. Christian theology and the Church have been the source of inspiration and support for many of the traditions of penology and the criminal law. As will be demonstrated below, such phenomena as the popular acceptance of criminal law as a moral code, belief in the absolute right of the state to punish, belief in the ultimate justness of punishment, and the practice of imprisonment itself, to name just a few, have derived no small measure of force and legitimacy from Christian thought and practice. The Christian roots of our legal and penal systems are still referred to as a kind of endorsement of their validity.

However, beliefs and practices born with good

1

intentions during an Age of Faith have all too often been distorted over time into self-sustaining cultural myths and institutions which are harmful to all who come into contact with them. Christians, as organized communities of believers, have abdicated to secular government responsibility for the administration of criminal justice. While lip-service is paid to "our great Judeo-Christian heritage" and values, there is little reflection of such a heritage in the modern functioning of the criminal justice system in America.

Yet despite this reality, Church leaders in America, until quite recently[1], have been all too willing to assume that the state's administration of criminal law and penology was compatible with fundamental precepts—that the torch of justice had been safely passed from Church to state. Other Christians, and Church leaders, ignoring the long historical involvement of Christianity in the development of our criminal justice system, steadfastly maintain that the Church has no right to "meddle in affairs of state".

To remedy this confusion about the responsibility of the Church, there is a need to distill the historical ingredients of penology in America—to determine the ways in which theological concepts have been used and abused in its development; to recognize the degree to which Christian thought and practice are responsible for the course which it has taken; to expose the subtle changes in its goals which have accompanied its development; and to point out the assumptions on which it rests.

Further, apart from the extensive history of Christian involvement, penology in America, by its very nature, presents significant challenges to Christian believers. For, penology is inextricably concerned with the same, vital, human issues which are so central to Christian belief. Every penal practice is necessarily based on a particular conceptualization of the human person—his nature, his rights, his destiny as a human being. Likewise, every penal practice involves implicit assumptions about the purpose of law and society, and what constitutes a proper standard for relations among human beings.

Christian revelation is certainly not silent on such issues. To the extent that Christians take seriously the judgment pronounced on the world by the Gospel, and also their obligation to face social and political reality as part of Christian life, then some confrontation with penal practice and belief is inevitable. Hence there is a need for examination of the compatibility of penology and Christian revelation and theology, before a clear sense of the Church's role in transforming criminal justice can emerge. On a practical level, it warrants recognition that the specific practices of any prison system stem from penal ideology, and for as long as the underlying assumptions and supporting ideology of the penal system remain unexamined and unchallenged, then that system will successfully resist all but the most superficial of changes.

Confusion over purpose also presents problems to Christians committed to working in criminal justice. Those who work in the penal system, in considering their identity and calling as Christians, must ask: to what degree am I an agent of the prison system and a supporter of its goals, and to what extent am I an agent in transforming it into a more Christian, more human institution? In the strained social atmosphere of the prison, questions of identity and allegiance assume a particular significance and Christians working there must be especially conscious of their purpose. For instance, what role should a chaplain play in maintaining order within the prison? Or, what concerns should motivate the Christian layperson who sits on a parole board? Or, what ethical challenges are presented to a prison guard or administrator by virtue of his position? While Christian reflection on penology would not necessarily seek to supply answers to specific questions, hopefully it would facilitate individuals' personal task of gaining perspective on their role within the penal system.

Finally, and most significantly, there is a compelling human argument for Christian concern over prisons, namely, the men and women who suffer from the tragedy of prisons are brothers and sisters of ours, and it is a Christian duty to assist them. Viewed as children of God, all people have a common birthright and likewise a common obligation to one another.

Traditionally, this justification for Christian involvement in prisons has been advanced in a limited, condescending form: Christians, "the saved", must rescue prisoners, "the sinners", by demonstrating to them the error of their ways, so that they might repent and "be saved". Aid to prisoners has largely been conceived of solely as a charitable work, a gratuitous act of Christians on behalf of the fallen.

This is not the argument advanced here, for such a justification for concern over prisons exhibits a shallow grasp of the real extent of the tragedy they represent. Certainly it cannot be denied that any viable Christian response to prisons must consider the individual tragedies of prison—the broken, often hopeless, and (properly defined) sinful lives of the prisoners themselves. However, at the same time prisons are equally, if not so obviously, destructive in the lives of those who build and support them, and the need for the existence of prisons is a sign of profound disorder in the structure of society which is (supposedly) protected by their operation. Contemporary American prisons do not just impose a judgment upon those whom they hold captive. Prisons likewise pronounce judgment on a way of life which relies upon their continuance, and tolerates the atrocities which routinely occur inside them. As Jessica Mitford has observed, the horrors of American prisons lend a sobering significance to the question: "Am I my brother's keeper?"[2] Christian involvement in prisons then is really a ministry to people on both sides of the wall, for there are many kinds of prisons.

Thus, the central problem this book is concerned with is: given the realities of criminal justice and penology in America, how should the Christian community of believers respond? Its overall objective is to consider in broad Christian perspective the issues raised by American criminal justice, as a tool for facilitating deeper Christian involvement.

The Relation of This Study to the Field of Theology

These reflections were not undertaken as a strict, academic study, in which theology is considered to be primarily an intellectual "science". Nor is this book concerned with the kinds of self-contained technical and theoretical issues which are the focus of so many theological works. Rather, it is a study of theology in the broad sense of the word. Nonetheless, despite its general character, there is a strong theoretical basis for this type of "theologizing", and this book draws its inspiration from several current trends in theological thought.

The project benefits from the re-discovery of "critical reflection" as a proper function of theological study. Latin American theologian Gustavo Guitierrez, who was instrumental in advancing this model, explains:

> Theology must be man's critical reflection on himself, on his own basic principles. Only with this approach will theology be a serious discourse, aware of itself, in full possession of its conceptual elements . . . But above all, we intend this term to express the theory of a definite practice. Theological reflection would then necessarily be a criticism of society and the Church insofar as they are called and addressed by the word of God; it would be a critical theory, worked out in the light of the word accepted in faith and inspired by a practical purpose—and therefore indissolubly linked to historical praxis.[3]

The concept of "praxis" is a crucial one. Defined, praxis is "the critical relationship between theory and practice, whereby each is dialectically influenced and transformed by the other".[4] Restated more simply, praxis is a two-edged sword. On the one side, it is concerned with the need for theology to focus on immediate, worldly issues, as much as it has traditionally focused on far-removed, doctrinal issues. On the other side, the concept of praxis maintains that by concerning itself with worldly reality, theology can play a vital role in affecting reality. The task of theology therefore, is to reflect upon human history and affairs, and through such reflection establish a means of approaching (and transforming) them in the future.

With respect to the focus of this study, criminal justice, critical reflection consists of a review of the history, ideology and practices of the American penal system, informed by this writer's involvement with that system over the past six years. It is "praxis theology" insofar as it is both grounded in real life experience with the criminal justice system and concerned with the possibilities for future transformation of that system.

Another theological trend which influenced this study is the modern concern that religious writing should reflect an accurate understanding of contemporary historical reality. German theologian Jurgen Moltman succinctly expressed this concern when he wrote:

> "Theology will always have to start from the fact that it speaks about the very reality of man that also confronts sociology. . . . If theology speaks at all about "the true man", destiny, justification, the demands made on man apart from his destiny, then its statements must be valid apart from faith. It must stand the test in the reality that has been entrusted to man".[5]

To illustrate, many Christian justifications for punishment of criminals are remnants of an age where Church and state were considered, if not identical, at least as working toward the same goals. The state was unquestioned as an ally of the Church and instrument of God's will. Today, however, we live in a secular age as opposed to a religious one, and traditional Christian justifications for punishment may well be inappropriate because they were formed in, and dependent upon, a different historical context. Thus, theology must be sensitive to its historical surroundings, or risk terrible error.

The Jesuit Karl Rahner has advanced similar concerns about theological reflection and the needs of individual believers. Rahner maintains: "Theological expressions are not formulated in such a way that they can see how it is that what is being said has any connection with their own understanding of themselves, which they have derived from their experience."[6] In short, theology often fails to adequately understand the human person and human experience. It was this failing of theology that led Rahner to his often quoted statement that: "Dogmatic theology today has to be theological anthropology."[7] More simply, Rahner is arguing that the exposition of Christian belief (dogmatic theology), must be accompanied by an exploration of the experience of human beings (anthropology) who are addressed and affected by that belief. "In every dogmatic question you examine you must seek to discover the conditions in man . . . which make it possible for him to arrive at knowledge of the matter in question."[8] For example, in American law, which evolved from the traditions of Western Christianity, both the definition of crime and justification for punishment are predicated on a belief in the individual as a free moral agent. It is assumed that the criminal willfully chooses to commit crimes, and therefore is deserving of punishment as a consequence. However, there is a great body of evidence which would indicate that many criminals do not freely act, or, in other cases, do not perceive themselves as being capable of free action. Consequently, traditional rigid formulations of free will may well prove to be inadequate as both theological and social models for understanding these individuals.

Yet Rahner's statement implies much more than this. For, to the extent that Christian theology is concerned with questions of anthropology, it does not take a neutral stance. Christian revelation makes definite statements about humankind. Thus while Christian anthropology is necessarily concerned with what is, it is likewise concerned with what *should be*. If the present reality in prisons is such that inmates cannot conceive of themselves as potentially free and responsible beings, then a Christian anthropology would function to extend the possibility of freedom to them. Or, if present official beliefs about prisoners are not sufficiently considerate of their human dignity and potentiality, then a viable Christian anthropology would serve to exert pressure to change those beliefs.

Finally, this study is influenced by recent arguments that theology must necessarily concern itself with *all* of human existence, if it is to have any real significance in the lives of Christians. As Bonhoeffer wrote, the entire world—all reality—must be "conformed to Christ", and Christianity should not be relegated to a small corner of personal existence.[9] If Christian belief is to be something vital in the modern world and not a superfluous remnant of an age past, it must face the challenge of secular culture in all its forms.

Returning to the subject of criminal justice, the penal system can be viewed as a crucible in which is tested the viability and significance of Christian belief. Or, perhaps a more appropriate analogy is that the tragedy of American criminal justice is a cup—to be accepted by the Christian community, or to be passed by. Needless to say, this study presumes that the cup should not be passed.

1
CHRISTIANITY AND THE EVOLUTION OF CRIMINAL LAW AND PENOLOGY

"Historical reflection", writes Moltmann, "begins where traditions have no longer kept pace with the present and are no longer experienced as being unquestionably 'obvious'."[1] Certainly our traditional methods of dealing with, and our attitudes toward, crime can no longer be considered as obviously right. Nor can we afford, given the current state of criminal justice in America, to uncritically embrace traditional Christian attitudes toward the problems of crime and punishment. On the contrary, the situation calls for thoughtful evaluation of traditional methods, and thus necessarily requires consideration of their historical evolution. This chapter then reviews the development of Western Christianity as it contributed to the growth of criminal law and penal practice.

Early Christianity

The very earliest Christian communities most likely had no conception of crime in a legal or social sense. Living in expectation of an impending second coming of Jesus, the first Christians did not see the regulation of social conduct in an organized way as a pressing concern.

Among early Christian sources, it would seem logical to seek clues about Christian attitudes toward crime in Jesus' command to visit prisoners. Such an approach would be misleading, however, for as British scholar A.E. Harvey observes; in New Testament times, "Prison was not regarded as a necessary element in the penal system and therefore in the administration of justice itself . . . It was essentially no different from the lot of a prisoner of war—and the same words are used in Hebrew and Greek for military, political and judicial prisoners. None of them had the connotation implicit in our word 'convict'."[2]

The first New Testament reference which seems to directly address the problem of crime in the community is Paul's letter to the Corinthians (I Cor., 6:1-11). In it, Paul berates the Christians for taking disputes to civil courts. "If one of you has a dispute with a brother, how dare he go before heathen judges, instead of allowing God's people settle the matter? . . . surely there is at least one wise man among your fellowship who can settle a dispute between the brothers." However, Paul also maintains that ideally, Christians ought to ignore crimes against them. "The very fact that you have legal disputes among yourselves shows that you have failed completely. Would it not be better for you to be wronged? Would it not be better for you to be robbed?" Peaceful resignation, rather than righteous indignation, was Paul's answer to crime.

Further insight into Christian attitudes toward offenders is provided by the Apostolic Constitutions, a collection of laws for governing the early Church.[3] While probably not composed until the year 380 A.D., they were based on a number of earlier sources and traditions stemming from the very first Christians. The

Constitutions repeat Paul's admonition not to take disputes to secular courts. "Let not the heathen therefore know of your differences among one another, nor do you receive unbelievers as witnesses against yourself, nor be judged by them, nor owe them anything on account of tribute or fear."[4] The Constitutions also repeat Paul's warning that legal disputes are undesirable. "If brethren have law suits with one another, which God forbid, you who are the rulers ought thence to learn that such as these do not do the work of brethren in the law, but rather of public enemies."[5] With regard to the problem of offenders in general, the Constitutions uphold the concept of a God who is both righteous and merciful. Offenses must not be ignored, yet offenders must not be condemned.

> "He will not acquit the guilty": though He welcomes the returning sinner, and revives him: leaving no room for suspicion to such as wish to judge sternly and reject offenders entirely . . . It therefore behooves you . . . to encourage those who have offended, and lead them to repentance, and afford them hope . . . Receive the penitent with alacrity, and rejoice over them, and with mercy and bowels of compassion judge the sinners.[6]

One of the more severe punishments prescribed for offenders is banishment from the community. Yet, Jesus' exhortation to forgive "seventy times seven" is explicitly restated, and Christians are required to accept penitent offenders "like fathers to children".[7]

Embodied in these various teachings about "crime" are particular elements of Christian belief which, over time, radically changed the way criminal offenses were viewed in the West. Most significantly, Christianity introduced the idea of personal morality, and its two foundations, free will and individual responsibility. Early criminal codes were largely "objective" in nature.[8] They focused upon the offense committed, as opposed to the offender, and prescribed set penalties for each crime, regardless of intent or circumstances. Murder, for instance, was usually penalized by the payment of a sum of money to the victim's surviving relatives, primarily to avoid blood feuds, or to appease the gods. There were no refined conceptions of relative degrees of guilt or personal moral standing; crime was simply one of the harsher realities in an already harsh world. This objective attitude toward crime was slowly changed by Christian influences.

. . . with (Christianity) arose the subjective attitude. While previously the law only recognized the injury to the individual or society—that is, the material crime in its direct relation (effect)—the ecclesiastical law looked to the soul of the man who had committed the crime. In its own language, its concern was that the soul had sinned, that it was to be healed, purified and regenerated through expiation and punishment.[9]

Christian teachers came to insist that the individual freely chose the course of action he/she followed. People were not forced to act in any given way; they decided what to do; they freely chose between good and evil. Relying upon this idea of free will, and New Testament teaching about the Final Judgment, Christian fathers taught that human beings were held responsible for their actions. Each individual was viewed as a unique entity, the author (with God) of his/her destiny. Therefore, each individual was accountable for his/her actions. And finally, given that humans were unique, free and responsible beings, they could be considered guilty for their actions and expected to make amends.

The ultimate impact of these ideas was to "spiritualize the notion of transgression".[10] Secular methods of approaching crime would no longer be centrally concerned with the offense itself; they would be more concerned with the offender. Likewise, crime came to be seen as necessarily an offense against God, and hence a concern of His people, the Church.

To summarize, several elements of early Christian thought on "crime" stand out: a spirit of peaceful resignation toward offenses and offenders, as opposed to one of zealous righteousness; concern with the spiritual implications of offenses against the community, not their social cost; and finally, emphasis on reconciliation of offenders with the community and with God.

Constantine and Theodosius – Church Immersion in the World

The early Church consisted of self-contained communities, struggling to survive in an often hostile world. They tried to avoid contact with secular government and affairs. The reign of the Emperor Constantine, however, was to radically change the relationship of Christians to the secular world, for, whatever his motivation, Constantine was determined not only to protect Christianity but to spread its influence throughout the Empire.[11]

Constantine sponsored a series of legislative acts

designed to secure a powerful position for the Church, and other laws supposedly reflecting Christian values. For instance, no slave could be branded upon the face for identification, since he/she was "fashioned in the image and likeness of God". Crucifixion as a means of execution was also abolished out of "reverence" for Jesus.[12] Interestingly, some of the more radical changes of Constantine's regime took place in the criminal law. As classical scholar Charles Cochrane observed:

> It is, perhaps, within the field of criminal law and procedure that the distinctive characteristics of the new regime most clearly emerge. In criminal jurisdiction the most remarkable features are the frequency of capital punishment, often of a peculiarly brutal character, the abolition of traditional offenses and penalties and the introduction of new ones, the use of legislation to improve moral and social conditions, with its inevitable concomitant, a growing confusion between the notions of crime and sin.[13]

Perhaps the most unusual act of all was Constantine's authorization of episcopal courts to engage in civil litigation.[14] By this step Constantine directly involved the Church in administering the law and in maintaining order in the Empire.

If Christianity and the Roman state were betrothed by Constantine they were married by Theodosius, who came to power a number of years after Constantine's regime. Theodosius, a Christian, issued a proclamation which required all Roman citizens to profess Christianity and categorized non-Christians as "madmen" and "heretics", "condemned as such, in the first instance, to suffer divine punishments, and, therewith, the vengeance of that power which we, by celestial authority, have assumed".[15] The Empire became fully committed to the advance of Christianity, by whatever means necessary, including employing legal sanctions against the so-called enemies of Christendom. The emperor assumed continually increasing status until finally his office was considered to be sacred. Many crimes against the emperor were no longer considered merely as social offenses but as sacrilege as well. Thus the merger of church and state, and the confusion between sacred and secular, sin and crime, which began under Constantine, advanced another step.

The result of this Church-state alliance was hardly the "baptism" of the Roman Empire. Rather it was abduction of the Christian faith to prop up a dying political and social order. As Cochrane insightfully concluded:

. . . For to envisage the faith as a political principle was not so much to christianize civilization as to "civilize" Christianity; it was not to consecrate human institutions to the service of God but rather to identify God with the maintenance of human institutions.[16]

This observation is doubly significant, for, with reference to the institutions of criminal justice, the same statement could be made about medieval Christianity and American Christianity well into the twentieth century. In the name of God, and in the protection of His "law", countless brutal and dehumanizing practices by political institutions have been justified.

The Church's alliance with the state was also important because it blunted Christians' critical attitude toward it. "The utilization of the state (by the Church) becomes the more important because less absolute standards and diminishing religious fervour soon produced a tendency to overlook the final worthlessness of the state, and because, on the other hand, the affinity of Christianity to the world, once it became an accepted fact, was bound to increase . . ."[17]

Yet, Church leaders often heroically confronted the state. Ambrose, Bishop of Milan, was not only vigilant about misuse of political power, he was also aware of the need to protect the weak and powerless from the oppression of criminal sanctions. In his book of instructions to the clergy, Ambrose wrote: "The regard in which one is held is also very much enhanced when one rescues a poor man out of the hands of a powerful one, or saves a condemned criminal from death . . . "[18] It is especially noteworthy, he adds, ". . . if one has freed a man who is crushed down by the resources and faction of a powerful person . . ."[19] In a later chapter, Ambrose recounts how he was subjected to criticism by Christians in his community for melting down gold to ransom criminals held prisoner.[20]

Augustine, a later contemporary of Ambrose, was known to frequently intervene in civil matters in an attempt to inject Christian values into legal and political matters. In one case, involving the murder of friends of his, Augustine wrote a letter to the judge which is one of the most remarkable witnesses to the Christian principle "love of enemies" ever recorded. Fearing a sentence of death, Augustine pleaded:

. . . by no means do this or permit this to be done. For although we might silently pass over the execution of criminals brought up for trial not by an accusation ours . . . we do not wish the sufferings of the servants of God avenged by the infliction of precisely similar injuries in the way of retaliation . . . Fulfill, Christian judge, the duty of an affectionate father; let your indignation against their crimes be tempered by considerations of humanity; be not provoked by the atrocity of their sinful deeds to gratify the passion of revenge, but rather be moved by the wounds which these deeds have inflicted on their own souls to exercise a desire to heal them.[21]

The Roman age produced a questionable alliance of Christianity with political power. Yet the best of Christian teaching retained its emphasis on the need for humaneness in dealing with offenders, and on reconciliation as the primary objective of any sanctions against them. Likewise, there is evidence that, in practice, Church courts were popular among the people because of their fairness and lack of brutality.[22] Thus, even though Christianity became allied with an often repressive social order, in its best moments it still identified with the powerless and oppressed, serving as their protector and as a sign of a new order to come.

The Middle Ages

Given the continual flux of social and political institutions in the Middle Ages, the relative stability and continuity of the Church made it a natural choice to provide both a sense of direction and some semblance of order in an otherwise unstable world.[23] In the early Middle Ages there were two notable Church contributions to the practice of criminal justice. The first was the emergence of the practice of the ordeal. Law was largely unknown, such that there was "great uncertainty in determining guilt or innocence and in establishing the validity of evidence".[24] There gradually evolved the custom of putting a witness or defendent to some physical test, the results of which would show whether they were truthful or not. For instance, the accused might be tied and thrown into water. If he or she floated to the top, it indicated guilt, ". . . for the pure nature of the water recognizes as impure and therefore rejects as inconsistent with itself such human nature as has once been regenerated by the waters of baptism and is again infected by falsehood".[25] Significantly, ordeals were always blessed by a mass, a special benediction or prayer, and were presided over by a priest. The ordeal was symptomatic of the belief that criminals were sinners against God and that evil was inconsistent with the very order of nature and hence would be exposed by physical trial. More importantly, God's judgment was believed to inflict punishment with divine approval. While the practice of inflicting ordeals gradually lost favor, the key underlying premise, that divine judgment is revealed in the working of human institutions, survived.

The second development of interest was monastic prisons. A system of monasteries, largely self-contained religious communities, dedicated to a prayerful and ascetic life and rigorous discipline as a means of salvation, spread across Europe in the early Middle Ages. One method of discipline which developed was that of imprisonment. Seventeenth century Benedictine monk Jean Mabillon[26] wrote about the first monastic prisons: "It appears that the place to which these penitents were condemned was more a retreat than a prison since there was a heated room and a workshop." However, eventually "a frightful kind of prison, where daylight never entered, was invented, and since it was designed for those who should finish their lives in it, received the name 'vade in Pace'."[27] In such prisons, the monks seldom heard mass; there were no visits, no words of consolation, except for "a superior who asks about their health without really acquainting himself with their needs and without seriously thinking of the means which would be necessary to make them return to God".[28] Monastic prisons were subject to frequent criticisms but infrequent reforms, and persisted almost until the eighteenth century.

Historically, these institutions signaled a change in the earlier Church attitude of compassion toward offenders. The lifelong isolation which was sometimes imposed showed little concern for reconciliation. The care previously evidenced by Christians toward the physical and spiritual well-being of offenders was missing. Finally, monastic prisons evidenced a preoccupation with a person's evil nature and sinfulness on the one hand, and God's vindictiveness and vengeance on the other. Monastic prisons at their worst were grounded in a hell-fire and damnation theology, which deemed it both necessary and proper to subject sinners to terrible suffering not so much in the hope of "saving them", as to inflict upon them "just" punishment for their sins. Interestingly, early American prison models bore a striking resemblance to monastic prisons, and were built upon almost identical theological premises.

The truly pivotal development of medieval times did not take place until the mid-twelfth century—the emergence of the Canon law. Around 1140 A.D., the monk Gratian produced a landmark collection of ecclesiastical law, providing the Church with a highly detailed, precise code for governing virtually all aspects of Christian life. The Code did not simply regulate Church affairs. It permeated all of medieval life.

> . . . The church, regarding itself as the greatest of all the civilizing institutions of the world, undertook many of the social and economic tasks which in modern times have come within the competence of the state. The scope of ecclesiastical legislation and judicature was extended far beyond the range of purely ecclesiastical matters . . .[29]

A large section of the Canon law was concerned with the criminal and disciplinary sanctions of the Church. The code formalized earlier Christian ideas about crime, especially free will and personal responsibility, and re-affirmed the link between the concepts of crime and sin. The Canon law taught that punishment of offenders was appropriate only insofar as they were morally guilty of offenses. By definition punishment could not simply be the infliction of some evil on an offender—it had to be the infliction of an evil justly incurred because of guilt.[30] Hence in assessing penalties the Church courts were greatly concerned with the relative degree of guilt of each offender. In determining guilt, Church courts would consider both the action of the offender—"actus reus", and whether or not he/she had a "guilty mind", evil intent—"mens rea". No offender could be subjected to punishment unless he/she were morally guilty by virtue of sinful intention. This concept was obviously a parallel to Church teaching on sin, whereby an individual must knowingly and wilfully commit an offense against God's law for an "actual sin" to exist.[31]

As Church thinking on crime grew "the Church went beyond the purely ecclesiastical sphere and entered the domain of lay jurisdiction in criminal cases; and, as an important aspect of its rise to a position of dominance in the medieval world, it ultimately acquired a jurisdiction which was truly criminal in character and so extensive in scope that it materially curtailed the criminal jurisdiction of medieval territorial states".[32] This expansion was in large part an attempt to seek the enforcement of moral values through external, coercive means.

Of course the Canon law prohibited the Church courts from imposing any punishment which would involve the shedding of blood, and (except for the Inquisition) from using torture in pursuing investigations. However, where execution was deemed the proper punishment, the Church prevailed upon secular government to prosecute and carry out the sentence. For instance, failure to execute a heretic would lead to a prince's automatic excommunication. The ban on capital punishment does not therefore seem to have been a genuine concern for criminals but rather a somewhat hypocritical attempt to keep the Church's hands technically free from blood, lest any guilt for the treatment of criminals be ascribed to it.[33]

Corresponding with increased Church involvement in temporal affairs, there resulted increasing acceptance of the law as an instrument of God's will.

Medieval literature is full of statements that God is the author of nature, the law or the beginning of

all law, the eternal and true law, the very truth
and the sun of righteousness . . . All positive law
is dependent upon eternal law, from which it
draws its authority, . . . secular law was considered a gift of God, and was felt to have a religious
sanction. For in the middle ages no easy distinction between law and morality was admitted . . .
It was an accepted fact that law in general remains
eternally the same and must rule unchallenged.[34]

Earlier Christian isolation from, or hostility toward, political power was suppressed by a new
philosophy which saw the state as both necessary and
an integral part of the "natural order" of existence.
Aquinas, for instance, saw government as allowing
man to fulfill his political and social nature, and as a
means whereby the morally and intellectually superior
rose to a position of leadership over the less gifted. He
viewed this as consistent with both "divine law" of
revelation and the "natural law" of God's creation.[35]
Aquinas' contemporary, Bonaventure, concluded that
the authority of the state was justified for negative
reasons—it served to constrain sinful humankind from
chaos and destruction.[36]

"From the end of the fifteenth century the growth
of temporal justice, at the expense of spiritual justice,
was ever more marked: one by one many of the subject
matters of the civil jurisdiction of the Church were
absorbed by the civil courts of temporal powers."[37]
Critically, the rise of secular authority and courts did
little to diminish the religious and moral overtones surrounding the administration of criminal justice. As
legal scholar Nicholas Kittrie wrote:

. . . crime and sin continued to be inextricably

merged . . . From the foggy interface of the state and church in this period evolved the concept that certain acts were punishable as crimes if they offended the temporal regimes represented by the Prince . . . The facility with which the sovereign's armies could be turned into police insured that thereafter offenders and punishments would be handled by the state. This transfer of functions, however, reflected little change in the public attitude that "God's will" was served by present and earthly punishment, a belief that provided both executioner and spectator with the feeling that they were directly involved in the 'Lord's work'.[38]

Nor was this sanctification of the state's purposes in punishing criminals in any way diminished by the Reformation. If anything, the state was endowed with even greater legitimacy. Martin Luther, in trying to reconcile the teaching of the New Testament with the political reality of his day, resorted to a dual system of public and private morality. "The work of government administration and punishment, including hanging, breaking on the wheel, and beheading, is all a service to God", just as much as "non-official purely personal morality" in which "the true service of God consists in loving one's enemies, in sacrifice, renunciation and endurance . . ."[39] Hence, Luther's followers would find no reason to question the brutal treatment of criminals in Christian ethics. John Calvin, the other great reformer, taught that the state and the law should be made use of by Christianity to promote both "the religious purpose of the maintenance of true religion; and the social and utilitarian end of the promotion of peace, order and prosperity".[40] Calvin's ideas would later be highly influential in shaping the early American experience.[41]

Criminals continued to be popularly conceived of as sinners, by virtue of the fact that the criminal law was still viewed as an extension of God's law. Consequently, the criminal law assumed an absolute character—it was uncritically accepted as the guardian of the moral order. Its severity and brutality from the late Middle Ages into modern times were legitimized by these beliefs.

Theologically, the medieval period saw the deemphasis, if not the loss, of the loving, conciliatory spirit which marked earlier Christian teaching about offenses. Contrast the judgmental tendency of Thomas Aquinas on heresey with the merciful spirit of Augustine centuries earlier:

> Heresy (writes Aquinas) is a sin which merits not only excommunication but also death, for it is worse to corrupt the faith which is the life of the soul than to issue counterfeit coins which minister to the secular life. Since counterfeiters are justly killed by princes as enemies to the common good, so heretics deserve the same punishment.[42]

Such sentiment is certainly a far cry from early Christian thought. Aquinas, however, was not being spitefully vindictive in writing these and other equally severe passages. Rather, his writing was a reflection of the theological understanding of his times. In medieval theology, the universe had a God-created order, a natural harmony. Law served to protect that order and punishment to restore it. The sinfulness of humankind and the very real threat of damnation played a central role in all of medieval life, and brutal punishments were then seen as necessary means of saving individuals' souls from hell-fire.

Tragically, the rigor and meticulous detail of medieval thought overshadowed the mysteries of God and human life. The early Christians' tentative struggling to understand their new faith, plus their willingness to experientially meet the Gospel, allowed for a latitude and humility which was reflected in their merciful ways with offenders. Whereas the medieval Christians' struggling to achieve near-absolute certainty in faith, coupled with their tendency to approach the Gospel in philosophical and abstract ways, resulted in a rigor and severity which was in turn reflected in their harsh treatment of offenders.[43]

Another cause of the de-emphasis of reconciliation in dealing with offenders probably was the Church's attempt to establish a Christian Kingdom on earth. The medieval goal of starting God's Kingdom in the realm of Christendom made the use of force ever more attractive, because physical coercion is apt to show more outward results in less time than spiritual persuasion. Thus the loss of a conciliatory spirit was to some degree sparked by an eschatological understanding of the Kingdom as existing without flaw on earth.[44]

Another medieval development was that the Church, which had introduced subjective considerations into the criminal law, ironically contributed to the gradual "depersonalization" of the concept of crime. In the early Christian tradition, offenses were always considered in terms of their interpersonal communal implications (in addition to spiritual ones). If one member of a Christian community offended against another, it was essential that they make peace and their relationship be restored. So important was communal harmony that the most severe punishment to an offender was banishment. In contrast, the central concern of medieval scholars and judges was that the natural order of creation or God's law, had been violated, and the proper balance must be restored. The focus shifted from the human to the abstract. Crime, as an idea, no longer represented the "injury" which one human being inflicts on another; rather, it primarily signified the violation of a metaphysical order. As the human element is lost, the possibilities for reconciliation between criminal and victim are lessened; the implications which criminal acts have for the larger community are obscured; and, belief in the criminal law as a moral standard or timeless truth, valid in and of itself, aside from whatever human price it exacts, is increased.

Next, medieval Christianity marked the decline of the Christian tradition of forebearance with offenders; the patient endurance of wrongs suffered. Via the Canon Law and Inquisition, the Christian spirit of resignation with regard to offenses against them was slowly replaced by one of zealousness, and seeds were sown for later popular equations of religious faith with overt moralism. This development of a "prosecutor's mentality" is highly ironic when one considers that among the early Christians, the "person of contentious spirit", who continually sought faults among brothers and sisters was severely rebuked, and the false accuser was exiled as "a murderer of his brother".[45]

A final medieval development which was a turning point in Christian history was the rise of legalism, which was both a cause and effect of the establishment of Canon Law. In subsequent theological discussion in both the Roman and Reformed Churches, the function and significance of law and authority in mapping out a narrow path for salvation were central themes. This served to instill in many Christians a natural deference to law and authority of any kind, and in the future sometimes inhibited criticism of secular government by Christians.[46] Likewise, the value which advocates of legalism placed on hierarchy and order, later provided a natural source of support for methods of administering criminal justice which had as their primary goal the efficient maintenance of social order.

The medieval heritage of Christian thought on law, crime and punishment remains influential today. The issues have remained as medieval Christianity defined them and while our theological understanding of God, the world and ourselves has greatly advanced in recent centuries, most Christian thought on crime and punishment is still decidedly medieval.

Medieval Christianity had significant influence over the subsequent evolution of civil government as well. First, even though the Church was no longer directly involved in the administration of criminal justice, the status of the criminal law as an extension of God's law, a moral code in and of itself, survived. The criminal law continued to be seen as the chief weapon in the fight between Good and Evil. Criminal law retained its original religious justification and legitimacy. Yet, at least in theory, there was a marked difference between Church and state goals in the administration of justice. As Mabillon saw in the seventeenth century: "In secular justice the principal purpose in view is to conserve and repair order and to instill fear into criminals, but in ecclesiastical justice one considers above all the welfare of the soul."[47] Restated, secular justice had political ends; Church justice, spiritual ends. When the end of Church involvement in criminal justice was not accompanied by popular recognition of these different functions of law, secular, political goals were disguised with religious justifications.

Related to this development was the rise of popular belief that the maintenance of social order was in accordance with divine will. The state became the protector of the good and moral values. "God-fearing" men would therefore ally themselves with the state and the prevailing social order. Given these assumptions, it followed that the state had a moral right to take extraordinary measures against criminals—those who were a threat to the prevailing order. Harsh and repressive punishments were therefore easily justified. The Church's tacit sanctioning of such methods, especially during the Inquisition, left it with little room for criticism of secular justice.

Finally, the popular conception of criminals which emerged from the Middle Ages was that they were wicked and depraved individuals, a threat to the common good. The emphasis on freedom of the will, which pervaded medieval thought, stressed that criminals were voluntarily malicious. Hence, criminals were not to be tolerated or pitied; they were to be eliminated.

In review, several observations suggest themselves. Christian teaching on crime and punishment is historically conditioned. It is not a consistent, timeless teaching progressing in linear fashion through history; it has changed to correspond with philosophical and historical developments. Given its historical relativity there exists no serious objection to a re-evaluation of Christian thought on crime. One challenge of faith to Christians in any age is to evaluate the historical situation in which they find themselves, and then to discern how revelation guides them in responding to that situation.[48]

Furthermore, history should make us suspicious of simplistic references to "our great Judeo-Christian" heritage in western law and penology. As was demonstrated, that heritage has yet to resolve its own internal contradictions and all too often religious allusions are employed not because political institutions reflect Judeo-Christian values, but because references to them are a convenient means of legitimizing prevailing practices. Church leaders who make such references, in order to support the Church's right to speak out on these issues, should be aware that they sometimes unwittingly imply approval of the status quo.

Finally, contemporary Christians should realize that the issues raised by criminal justice are questions of vital Christian concern. Christians have been all too willing to concede that crime and punishment were the sole concerns of the state, in which they should not meddle. Some Christians have concluded that the modern, "scientific" approach to criminal behavior has made Christian teaching on crime obsolete. Still others, ignoring the gradual process of evolution which produced the criminal law, assume that modern codes are strictly "scientific" or "objective" in nature, and that Christian reflection on law and penology is no longer meaningful. Nonetheless, Christian silence on issues of criminal justice in no way eliminates our responsibility to speak on these issues.

2
PENAL MODELS IN THE AMERICAN EXPERIENCE

Throughout American history, various "answers" to the "problem" of crime have been advanced in the form of penal models for dealing with convicted criminals. Most were hailed as *the* solution for stopping crime. Yet, each has been little more than a shooting star, flaring confidently with initial promise, only to disappear, scattering remnants behind. This chapter is a brief history of the major models and trends in American penal practice. Its focus is not so much the specific conditions and practices of American prisons, as it is the philosophy, purpose and anthropology on which they are based; and the role which organized religion and theological concepts have played in their development.

Puritan and Quaker Roots

The roots of American penology are found in the contrasting views toward crime and punishment held by Puritan and Quaker colonists. The Puritans viewed themselves as "a sacred remnant people, establishing an ideal commonwealth", based on their Christian faith. They used law to advance their religious beliefs, to punish those who denigrated those beliefs, and to enforce what they believed to be proper standards of moral behavior. The intermingling of the ideas of crime and sin which was so characteristic of the Middle Ages was revived in Puritan America and criminal penalties were attached to a number of "offenses against religion"; such as blasphemy, idolatry, speaking against the bible, etc., in addition to "traditional" criminal offenses such as murder or robbery.

A Calvinist emphasis on the innate depravity of all human beings, and the continual need for authority to keep them from temptation, made the criminal law a singularly important institution in Puritan society. Man-made laws were seen as a way to extend the Ten Commandments to society:

> . . . the authority of the bible served as justification for the provisions of the law. The law was God's enacted word on earth . . . Authority of the state was thus religiously condoned. Carried to its conclusion, this meant that the welfare of the whole, rather than of the individual, was the chief concern of the state.[1]

Of course it followed that violation of the law was a serious matter; and offenders could suffer severe penalties, the worst being death. Punishment had several purposes in the Puritan approach to crime. Reformation of the offender, however, was not one of them. All men were seen as being inherently sinful and evil in their ways. Criminals were simply extreme representations of the evil tendencies in all human beings. Only God could save human beings from their sinfulness; by themselves they were powerless. The notion that criminals, whose disfavor in God's eyes was apparent in their lowly social status, could be dissuaded from evil, or reformed, was logically absurd. Punishment therefore was not as a rule seen as being reformatory. Rather, punishment was justified as protection of the community by publicly exposing the sinner, and as a warning to all of those present to resist temptation so as to not follow the sinner into public humiliation and shame or even death.[2]

The Puritans were strongly influenced by the talionic aspects of the Old Testament—"an eye for an eye" . . . "a life for a life". The Puritan society, self-proclaimed as representing God's will on earth, assumed the right to represent His justice in their punishment of criminals. Furthermore, unless criminals were punished, it implied indifference on the part of the community and acceptance of their acts.

The religious significance of criminal punishment, particularly execution, is captured in the practice of the "execution sermon". While the condemned man stood upon the gallows, facing his coffin, a minister would preach on a subject appropriate to the occasion. Unless crime were punished, one Puritan preached, "the judgments of God shall fall upon this land".[3]

On the other hand, the Quakers took a radically different approach to crime and punishment. Law for them was not the central concern that it was for the Puritans, and their tolerant spirit diminished the need for severe punishment to ensure religious and moral conformity. Hence, as a substitute for the English system of corporal and capital punishment, they instituted a system of prisons and workhouses to which offenders could be sentenced.

The Quaker penal model was an explicitly religious one, patterned after the prison visitation model of the early Christians who "had concerned themselves with the spiritual and bodily welfare of captives and prisoners . . ." and whom "the Quakers strove so zealously to imitate".[4] The Quakers abandoned the prevailing penal theory of their time, vindictive punishment, to establish a humane approach to criminal punishment characterized by an acute concern for individual offenders. "As a human being, with human sensibilities, the convict has a right to expect a wholesome place to live in . . . Further, the convict has a right to be protected against injury not only to his health, but to his moral life as well."[5]

Whereas the Puritans had conceived of criminals as being innately evil and beyond any hope of change, the Quakers steadfastly believed that crime did not originate with the individual offender, but rather had its roots in society at large and the environmental influences to which the criminal had been exposed. Via the punishment of isolation and hard labor, the Quakers hoped that individuals would be freed from contaminating influences, repent for their crimes, and be restored to fellowship with God and humanity. Implicit in the Quaker model was a belief that there was something sacred in every individual. Each criminal was to be considered an end in himself or herself, not a means for preserving the social order. (Typifying this spirit, one Quaker called execution a "blot upon religion").[6] Another Quaker assumption was that because of a basic unity among all people, society had a responsibility toward criminals as fellow human beings. The Quakers had "a conception of the criminal as at least partially a victim of conditions created by society and that he therefore had certain claims upon this same society", with society "under moral obligation to do what it could toward his reform".[7]

The harsh Puritan and humane Quaker ideas provide the backdrop for American penal history.[8] Hardline, repressive attitudes toward crime continually clash with more liberal views, never resulting in a consensus of what to do about crime. And while the historical context changes, the basic questions with which the Puritans and Quakers grappled remain the same through subsequent times, even to today.

The Penitentiary Movement

Widespread use of imprisonment as a means of punishing criminals did not begin until the colonies had achieved independence from Britain. In the period immediately following the American revolution, there arose a movement to re-design the penal system; to develop a home-grown method to replace the system left by the British.[9] The leadership for these developments came from Philadelphia, the center of intellectual activity in the new nation.

A number of religious denominations formed a Society for the Alleviation of the Miseries of Public Prisons, better known as the Pennsylvania Prison Society, which focused attention on prisons as a social institution which could be transformed into a humane and morally acceptable method for dealing with convicted criminals; and a means whereby they could be not only reformed but converted and "saved".[10] The overtly religious significance of criminal law and punishment was no longer as prevalent as it had been in the Puritan or the Quaker societies. But the actual regimen of the new prisons, ranging from the program of morals instruction, to the committees of ministers which inspected the prisons, to the explicitly religious model of repentance which was the basis for solitary confinement, reflected the strong Protestant religious influence of the times. "So firmly did the reformers believe that Christian faith was necessary to bring about the reformation which they were seeking that they used . . . every means possible to promote moral and religious improvement in the prison".[11] Thus, in the new nation, Church and state were still allied in the fight against crime. The practice of imprisonment, based in large part on religious models, grew and flourished as a result of Christian support. As one historian expressed it: "This coalition of Protestants was able to implement the ideals of pietism within living political institutions. If its soul was Quaker, its body, at least, was Calvinist."[12]

The most notable development in early American penology was the penitentiary, and its use of solitary confinement. The key underlying premise of the penitentiary concept as it evolved in the Pennsylvania prisons is best stated by one of the penitentiary's Morals Instructors:

> The utmost that can be claimed for any reformatory system of punishment is its predisposing influence to serious reflection . . . The power of Divine Grace we know can effect a change in the heart of any man under any circumstances, and God always works by means adapted to the end; but so long as 'evil communications corrupt good manners'; the association of evil men places an almost insuperable obstacle to moral improvement of the already corrupted. The separation of convicts removes that obstacle.[13]

Or, as the penitentiary approach was described by sociologist David Rothman: "Convinced that deviancy was primarily the result of the corruptions pervading the community, and that organizations like the family and the church were not counterbalancing them, they believed that a setting which removed the offender from all temptations and substituted a steady and regular regimen would reform him. Since the convict was not inherently depraved, but the victim of an upbringing that had failed to provide protection against the vices at loose in society, a well-ordered institution could successfully re-educate and rehabilitate him."[14] The convict was permitted to see no one save the warden of the prison or the Morals Instructor. Permission to work was granted to convicts not to ease the burden of loneliness or boredom, but for "acquisition by the convicts of habits of industry" and "the contribution by the convict through industry to the expense of maintaining the prison".[15]

The Morals Instructor's task was to "attend to the religious and moral instruction of the convicts in such manner as to make their confinement, as far as possible, the means of their reformation, so that when restored to liberty, they may prove to be honest, industrious and useful members of society".[16] Significantly, religion was seen as a means whereby individuals can be convinced to conform to the larger society and obey demands of the state. It should thus not be surprising that inmates who failed to respond to the persuasion of the Morals Instructor might be subjected to persuasion of a different kind:

. . . when, as punishment to a sturdy and disorderly convict, the Warden has ordered the light of his cell to be closed, a little time has elapsed with the most hardy before a prisoner has been found broken down in his spirit, and begging for hard work and his Bible to beguile the tedium of absolute idleness in solitude . . . work and moral religious books are regarded as favours and are withheld as punishment.[17]

In short, the Pennsylvania system evolved into a system of conversion by coercion—repent or else!

In the early eighteenth century a rival to the Pennsylvania system was born in New York state, which was to vie with the Pennsylvania system for dominance in American penology throughout the century. The (New York) Auburn system, also known as the "silent system", prohibited communication between inmates, and required hard labor. It differed, however, in that it allowed inmates to work together (in silence) in shops, "in order to take advantage of industrial machinery and organization as in a factory in free society". This congregate system of work with silence was enforced by corporal punishments and generally harsh discipline to facilitate the easy control of the prisoners. As historian Orlando Lewis observes, the Auburn system was an "insurgent and reactionary movement against the failure of the first prison system . . . a system replete with severity, regularity, perpetual silence and the domination by the prison authorities of the inmate's body and spirit".[18]

The Auburn system advanced the same goal as the Pennsylvania system—the reformation of the prisoner through penitence, but the Auburn advocates claimed to have a more effective, and of greater significance, a more efficient means of achieving this goal. One belief of the Auburn system was that leaving inmates in cells by themselves did not necessarily hasten or encourage their repentance. It was necessary to dominate them, to conquer them, before they could be safely returned to society. Hence, a number of practices designed to add to prisoners degradation and shame were invented, including shaved heads, striped uniforms, etc., all of which serve as a constant reminder to the inmate that he was not fit to associate with decent human beings. As Elam Lynds, a famous warden of Sing Sing prison in New York maintained: "In order to reform a criminal you must first break his spirit."[19]

In addition to the systematic degradation of prisoners, the Auburn system introduced the sentencing of inmates to prison for hard labor. The ingrained American cultural faith in the Protestant "work ethic" simply couldn't allow the possibility of prisoners avoiding work during captivity. As Orlando Lewis summarized the popular sentiment: "Was it not an edict from on high that man must earn his bread through the sweat of his brow? Was there any reason why men in prison should not work at least as hard as the honest, God-fearing supporter of a family on the outside?"[20] Gradually the entire focus of the system came to be efficiency, not reformation of the individual offender.

> The "agent and Keeper" was the business manager of the institution. Reformation was not his duty. Frequently he doubted that it could be achieved . . . These officials were not concerned with the saving of prisoners' souls but with the security of their bodies and the protection of citizens from their depradation.[21]

In the Auburn system, chaplains were "tolerated rather than actively favored by the administration".

This toleration took the form of making the chaplain, to a large extent, merely the arm of the keeper. "The chaplain was to conform strictly to all the rules of the prison. He was to give no hope or promise of pardon, or of attempting to procure a pardon . . . He was to make the convict feel the necessity of amendment and of strict obedience. He was to convince, if possible, the convict of the justness of his sentence."[22] But, chaplains apparently did not object to their diminished influence over the system. In fact, they seemed to support the Auburn methods and were grateful for the discipline which it afforded. In reference to harsh corporal punishment, Auburn's chaplain wrote in one annual report that it would be "most unfortunate . . . if the public mind were to settle down into repugnance to the use of such coercive means . . . Only relax the reins of discipline . . . and a chaplain's labors would be of no more use here than in a drunken mob".[23]

The Pennsylvania and Auburn systems competed through the first half of the eighteenth century for dominance in American penal thought and practice. Ultimately, however, faith in the underlying assumptions of the penitentiary dissolved and the penitentiary survived only as a physical plant for the confinement of inmates.

> (With) large-scale non-English immigration . . . and allegedly inferior races appearing in the penitentiaries, the sustaining belief in the reformability of the inmate waned. All that was left . . . was the order of solitude and labor. In the penitentiary system, the inmate was rendered unsocial. But that was supposed to be a means to the end of reformation. When the end collapsed, the means

survived, and the prisons continued to try to cut the inmate off from his social roots.[24]

So it is that the large grey stone buildings, the penitentiaries of the eighteenth century, survive to this day.

In retrospect, several reasons for the failure of the penitentiary become clear. Not the least of these is that the movement represented an uncritical, widespread application of a highly specific, religious concept, penitence, to a wide range of social problems where it simply did not apply. Whatever the real inspiration of the penitentiary reformers, whether it was the medieval monastic prison, or just a general religious feeling that sinners must be brought to repentance, they naively assumed that it was possible to generalize from a specific religious model in order to devise a universally applicable means of solving the problem of crime.

The reformers gave little thought to the difficulties involved in trying to remain true to an altruistic, religious ideal within the context of political and social reality. They apparently did not foresee how easy it would be for political authority to distort the original goal of penitence for reformation's sake, in order to make use of the harsh discipline of the penitentiary as a means of maintaining social order. Nor did they evidence qualms that the infliction of such suffering on criminals was unjust, despite the fact that social influences were recognized as being largely responsible for the existence of crime. Rather, a blind religious faith in the power of their ideas, or in other cases, a broad cultural faith in the righteousness of American political and social institutions and the American way of life, led the advocates of penitentiaries to support the institution uncritically and to endorse its effect upon criminals.

Moreover, despite its religious justification, the reformers' model of punishment and penitence was, in fact, significantly different from that of the medieval Church. For the Church's approach to punishment and repentance, at least in theory (The Inquisition and the worst monastic prisons were the major exceptions.), was based on the belief that penances (punishments) were effective only when the sinner had voluntarily repented. The power of human freedom made it impossible to compel someone to feel truly repentant for sin. Repentance must be a free act of the will; otherwise, it would not be the result of sorrow and remorse, but of fear or self-interest. Punishment was something which *followed* repentance, as a penance, a sign of purification and resolve not to sin again. The spiritual value of a penance not performed voluntarily was slight. The penitentiary model reversed this order. Punishment was to precede and lead the sinner to repentance. The sinner *must be made* to repent. What the penitential reformers failed to recognize, however, was the power of the human will, and the absurdity of trying to force offenders into true repentance by denying them liberty. Ironically, while the penitentiary denied prisoners' physical freedom, and had deleterious psychological effects, it failed to eradicate their most important freedom—freedom to resist spiritual coercion.

Defenders of the penitentiary could have profitably read Benedictine Jean Mabillon's criticism of harsh monastic prisons which were supposed to have led monks to repentance:

May no one say that it is good for them to be left alone in order to get time to think about their conscience and seriously reflect upon the sad state into which they have precipitated themselves. Far

from that . . . they are usually incapable of feeling
the charm of the state of grace under such conditions, nothing being more opposed thereto than
the excess of sadness which overwhelms them
and causes them to sigh under the burden of their
past sins . . . This is why one sees so little fruit
from the prisons and penances . . . and why these
poor unfortunates so often lose their mind or all
sensitiveness; . . . that they become insane or
hardened and desperate.[25]

In the American penitentiary experiment, when the
administrators of the prisons saw that the prisoners
were not repenting, but were rather becoming "hardened and desperate", they apparently abandoned hope
of spiritual coercion and settled for physical and psychological domination in its place.

Aside from inadequate understanding of the nature of repentance on which it was based, the penitentiary system also failed because it rested upon the false
assumption that the best means to restore criminals to
society was to completely cut them off from contact
with society. Certainly there was a peculiar logic to the
penitentiary system: if social influences corrupt, corruption can be stopped by eliminating all social contact. Yet such reasoning was tragically blind to one of
the fundamental truths about human beings—we are
social beings who live through interrelationships with
others. To assume that reformation could take place in
a situation where all human contact and interpersonal
relationships were cut off, assured that the penitentiary movement would inevitably fail to restore offenders to the community. Again Mabillon's criticisms
were prophetic: "By experience one knows but too

well that it is sufficiently hard to pass only a few days in silence and spiritual exercises which are voluntarily done, . . . And yet one imagines that poor wretches, overwhelmed by shame and sorrow, could pass entire years in a narrow prison without conversation and human consolations?"[26]

Finally, penitentiaries were a failure because over time the reformers who had initiated their construction, and who were motivated by genuine religious and humanitarian concerns, however mistaken their methods, were replaced by "keepers" with no particular religious or ethical concern for those in their charge. As with most movements, however, gradually interest waned and Christians and "men of good will" found other outlets for their philanthropic instincts. The penitentiaries continued, but they were "no longer buttressed by the social context and the psychological presuppositions which called them forth".[27] They were pseudo-religious institutions, retaining a religious title, a cathedral-like exterior, and monastic cells, but the individuals responsible for these innovations, and their good intentions, had since become history.

The Reformatory Movement

In 1870, prison officials, penologists, ministers and others concerned with the American system of penology gathered in Cincinnati for the first Congress of the National Prison Association (now known as the American Correctional Association). Motivated by the apparent failure of American prisons as well as the advent of new ideas in penology, the Congress drafted a Declaration of Principles, which remains in effect as a standard for American prisons to this day. Among other things, this Declaration proposed "the objective of 'moral regeneration' of the prisoner as opposed to 'vindictive suffering'; classification of criminals 'based on character' as determined by their progress in prison; and the indeterminate sentence under which the offender would be released as soon as the 'moral cure' had been effected and 'satisfactory proof of reformation' obtained".[28]

The Congress exhibited a rather peculiar intermingling of the religious fervor of earlier systems and the deterministic, scientific approach of the criminological revolution. Thus, on the one hand, the keynote speaker argues that: "Granite walls and iron bars, although they deprive the criminal of liberty and inflict a just physical punishment, do not work that reformation in the soul of the man that will restore him to society regenerated and reformed", and on the other hand, a later speaker maintains "A criminal is a man who has suffered under a disease evinced by the perpetration of a crime . . ."[29]

The net result of this first Congress was the rise of the reformatory, which unlike the prison, was not to be a place of punishment, but a place where the individual criminal would be reeducated in order to re-enter society as a productive member. The prototypical American reformatory was Elmira Reformatory in New York, model for the "Elmira System". It incorporated a modernized physical plant, a "liberal prison dietary" and adequate medical care in its operation. For reformation, there existed a wide variety of educational/ vocational programs, a library, an institutional newspaper, planned recreation and religious services.[30]

At first Elmira and other reformatories were greeted with much acclaim by penal authorities. Yet, in

1871, just one year after the Declaration of Principles, the United States Supreme Court ruled that a prisoner "not only forfeited his liberty, but all his personal rights except those which the law in its humanity accords him. He is for the time being a slave of the state".[31] At the same time, the American public was not at all interested in safeguarding the rights of prisoners. As Lawrence Friedman documents in his study on American law:

> Somehow reforms never took hold; or were perverted in practice. The fact is that convicts, like paupers and blacks, were at the very bottom of American society; . . . People detested crime, and were afraid of it. They wanted criminals punished, and severely; even more, they wanted bad people kept out of sight and circulation. Despite the rhetoric, the evidence of what men did shows that they considered it more important to warehouse, quarantine, and guard the "criminal class" than to cure them of their habits.[32]

In short, the reformatory movement was a pronounced failure,[33] and as Barnes concluded "has had little effect upon either the construction or administration of prisons for adults".[34]

The reformatory movement is not of interest in and of itself. Its importance stems from the fact that it foreshadowed the major movement of twentieth century penology, the introduction of "treatment" models in prisons. In considering reformatories, American penal authorities took official notice of the trend in criminology to view crime increasingly in psychological and medical terms as opposed to religious or moral ones. The reformatory movement also foreshadowed the new role which religion was to play within the penal system. Significantly, many of the participants in the NPA Congress which drafted the new declaration were clergymen and Christian philanthropists. As the Rev. F.H. Wines concluded: "Let us then, go . . . to toil faithfully, resolutely, persistently, in our respective fields of labor, and so to fulfill the high mission assigned us by Providence—the regeneration and redemption of fallen humanity."[35] Certainly, the motivation was still pre-eminently religious. But careful "scientific" programs of education and recreation, combined with control over environmental influences in the institution, were to be the means of affecting reform. Thus a spirit of liberal Protestantism, which viewed political and social institutions as tools in the hands of Christian believers, provided a new endorsement of imprisonment as a legitimate, thoroughly Christian institution, as American penology moved into the twentieth century.

The Twentieth Century—Rehabilitation/Treatment

Discontent with the American penal system grew as its ineffectiveness became more apparent:

. . . by the beginning of the twentieth century a realization of the inefficiency of this system of deterrence by long penal servitude as an effective means of protecting society against crime began to be felt and became demonstrable . . . The last fifty years have witnessed a critical evaluation of the utility to society of these successive systems . . . There has evolved from this experience the thesis that a more workable way to protect society is to fit the treatment to the individual, not the punishment to the crime.[36]

So the treatment model arrived in the American prisons.

Treatment, or rehabilitation, is a very loosely defined term which includes "everything from group counseling and psychotherapy to the teaching of eighth grade arithmetic, to putting TV sets in recreation rooms, to the kindness implied in the phrase 'we treat them well here'."[37] Despite this ambiguity, certain assumptions are common to virtually all treatment programs. Most incorporate as a prominent element the idea that criminality is essentially a psychological problem, caused by emotional or environmental forces. In extreme forms, the inmate is, in a classical psychiatric sense, considered to be "sick". Thus former Attorney General Ramsey Clark writes: "Most people who commit serious crimes have mental health problems,"[38] or, Dr. Karl Menninger concludes that crime signifies the "spasms and struggles of a submarginal human being".[39]

In the treatment model, criminals are conceived of as determined human beings, who did what they did because of uncontrollable impulses or unconscious motivations. Nicholas Kittrie cites as an example a psychoanalyst's explanation of crime:

Criminality presupposes specific childhood conflicts and their insolubility . . . In many instances the social factor in crime is either an excuse or a rationalization for hidden unconscious motives. The focal point of the criminal act is the repetition of injustices experienced in reality or fantasy in the child-mother (later, father) relationship, projected and perpetuated masochistically upon society.[40]

In short, crime occurs because of the existence of determining psychological factors in the mind of the individual. In the treatment model, a criminal is properly conceived of as a patient or client who needs to be cured. Ideally therefore, prisons are not places where punishment takes place. Rather, according to treatment theorists, a parallel can be drawn between prisons and hospitals as institutions where "cures" are effected. Accordingly, it is both ineffective and unjust to punish criminals, for they are not fully-functioning human beings and therefore cannot be held accountable for their actions.

With the treatment movement, there arose a call for a system of indeterminate sentences, whereby convicts would be kept in prison for an unspecified period of time, until their reformation was deemed complete. Previously, criminal sentences had been set for a specified period of time—a criminal sentenced to serve five years for robbery actually served five years. Among other things, increasing use of the indeterminate sentence gave prison authorities great coercive power over the prisoners, because they exercise great influence over the date of their release. Likewise, the indeterminate sentence has been used to force inmates to participate in treatment programs against their will. For instance, one black youth convicted of assault, with a maximum sentence of five years served six years in a Maryland treatment institution because he refused to participate in treatment programs, until he was released by a decision of the United States Supreme Court.[41]

The rise of the treatment model in prisons gave rise to many changes in rhetoric and terminology as well. Prisons became "correctional institutions"; guards became "correctional officers"; and inmates were renamed "residents" or "clients". The purpose of the system was no longer to be punishment, but "rehabilitation" or "resocialization". Solitary confinement and punishment cells became "administrative segregation" and "adjustment centers", etc.

Treatment goals are vaguely defined. Basically, the chief objective can be summarized as having the inmate, "client", accept the behavioral patterns and value systems of society at large. One specific objective is to persuade the prisoner to accept his status both within prison and in society. The *Manual of Instruction for Group Leaders* in the California State prison system has as its first goal: "To help prisoners adjust to the frustrations that are an unalterable part of life in an institution and in society."[42] Psychiatrist Thomas Szaz has pointed out that "mental health and illness are but new words for describing moral values. More generally, the semantics of the mental health movement is but a new vocabulary for promoting a particular kind of social ethic".[43] In the prison context, this has come to mean the inmate's accepting the social and cultural values of the treatment and custodial staff of the institution where he is incarcerated, and often his conforming to the expectations of the parole board as well.

In the treatment model, criminals are conceived of as being different from "normal" human beings by virtue of their psychological or emotional state—they are no longer seen as morally inferior but rather as psychologically inferior. "Phrases like 'inadequate personalities', 'borderline sociopaths', 'weak super-egos' come trippingly off the tongue of the latter-day prison warden, having long since replaced the sin-stained souls and fallen men or women with whom his predecessor had to cope."[44] Convicts are viewed as being intractable by themselves and must be "motivated" to take advantage of rehabilitative oppor-tunities. Thus, treatment involves an interesting paradox—on the one hand the inmate is conceived of as incapable of responsible human action because his or her behavior is determined, yet at the same time he/she is subjected to a program which is intended to obtain his or her "voluntary" allegiance to the princi-ples and values of the larger society.

With some exceptions, the treatment model grew not from excessive concern for the individual inmate, but rather from concerns for social defense. As Profes-sor Kittrie noted:

> This evolution (to treatment) is couched in highly pragmatic terms. It suggests that the recent at-titudes toward treatment of offenders spring from an objective determination that brutality, terror, and mechanistic rules do not serve the primary goals of our penal system—social defense. In this modern search for social defense the traditional techniques for accomplishing order and confor-mity . . . assume new perspectives.[45]

From another perspective, while earlier penal models had asserted the unequivocal right of the state to punish as a means of obtaining social goals, the more recent treatment model assumes the unequivocal right of the state to "treat" as a means of obtaining those same goals. Thus American penal history consists of an advance from the religious to the secular to the therapeutic state. However, as inferred above, the differences between the models are not quite so pronounced. In Thomas Szaz' ironic analogy:

> Modern psychiatric ideology is an adaptation—to a scientific age—of the traditional ideology of Christian theology. Instead of being born into sin, man is born into sickness. Instead of life being a vale of tears, it is a vale of diseases. In short, whereas in the Age of Faith the ideology was Christian, the technology clerical, and the expert priestly; in the Age of Madness the ideology is medical, the technology clinical and the expert psychiatric.[46]

Optimism about treatment among prisoners and penologists did not survive for long. Treatment ideals were never fully implemented. It is estimated that nation-wide only about five percent of money spent for penal programs was actually spent for treatment purposes. Another problem with the treatment approach was the inherent absurdity of attempting to create a therapeutic environment in what was ultimately a punitive institution. Frequent clashes between custody staff (guards) and treatment personel were as a rule decided in custody's favor. Writing in 1950, the real beginning of widespread treatment efforts in American prisons, a prison psychiatrist maintained that the treatment model could never succeed because the prison system by its very nature was more concerned with security and the repression of prisoners rather than any therapeutic goals.[47]

In this regard the disciples of treatment made the same basic error as the early "apostles of penitentiaries". They naively assumed that a basically humanitarian therapeutic ethic could be transplanted to a basically repressive social and political institution and not be perverted in the process. Also, as the penitentiary advocates believed that physical punishment would ultimately lead one to repentance and reformation, so treatment supporters believed that threats such as the indeterminate sentence and the withholding of privileges would ultimately result in psychological transformation.

Treatment also failed because, despite the rhetoric, inmates soon perceived that most prison administrators still regarded prisons as punitive institutions where security was the paramount concern, and that treatment was in most cases little more than a subtle, scientific form of coercion as a substitute for former physical coercion such as whippings and water tortures. A 1966 study found that seventy percent of the inmates polled viewed treatment as "phony" or "games".[48] Also, as John Irwin reported:

> Inmates have reacted to the sickness image of themselves which underpins the treatment ideal. This view that they are emotionally disturbed has proven to be less dignified and more humiliating than that of moral unworthiness. At least the morally depraved are considered responsible for their own actions, whereas the emotionally disturbed are considered incapable of wilfull acts.[49]

The treatment model, like the earlier penitentiary,

underestimated the human power of freedom to resist coercion. The resistance of modern prisoners to treatment methods, however, has been far more sophisticated, and has shown far more consciousness of what is actually happening to them, than did the resistance of the inmates of earlier penitentiaries. Whereas before prisoners often displayed resistance by being sullen and refusing to cooperate with their jailers except under the threat of the whip, contemporary prisoners have used their relatively greater physical freedom to directly challenge what is happening to them in the courts, in publications and in organized protests within institutions.

Gradually, officials took notice of the failure of treatment programs. The most frightening result of the failure of treatment has been the rise of behavioral modification experiments which were designed to forcibly change prisoners' behavior patterns. James Robinson, a researcher for the California Department of Corrections explained it: "The latest reasoning is that it's costly and inappropriate to go the psychotherapy route with these people . . . Instead, we'll focus on their deviant behavior and force them to shape up . . . henceforth the slogan will be 'they must be made to behave'."[50]

Means proposed for making prisoners behave included modified brainwashing, the object of which is to destroy all of the prisoners' values and social contacts and replace them with new ones; sensory deprivation, which would lower a prisoner's psychological resistance and make him susceptible to propaganda urging him to "reform"; chemotherapy, which consists of using drugs such as anti-testosterone hormones to chemically castrate prisoners; aversion therapy, in which pain or fear would be medically induced to threaten prisoners into "reform"; and psychosurgery, which would involve cutting or destroying areas of the brain which are supposedly related to violent behavior.[51] Each of these methods has apparently been tried on prisoners at some time, although they have not achieved widespread acceptance. It was notably in the federal prison system during the Nixon administration and in the California prisons that these methods were advocated. Widespread public outcry against such methods has helped to prevent their spread, but it is still unclear how extensive such experiments are within the American penal system and what their future will be.

Throughout the twentieth century, organized religion and overt expressions of Christian principles were much less evident. Among Christians, it was generally accepted that imprisonment represented a proper exercise of government's power to enforce laws and punish, and that such governmental action fostered creation of a more Christian (i.e. orderly and "moral") society. Religion was conceived of as a force for inculcating moral values and good habits in the private lives of individuals. To be a good Christian was to be socially acceptable—hold a job, support a family, attend Church, be patriotic, and avoid such sinful habits as heavy drinking, cursing, gambling, etc., which would tend to lead one into a life of crime. Logically then, the cause of crime was often pronounced to be a lack of religious and moral training. Numerous studies were undertaken to discover a link between lack of church affiliation or belief in God, and criminality.[52] However, when the studies showed that the vast majority of prisoners already had formal religious training or affiliation with a church, Christians were quick to find other causes for crime and to lose interest in promoting religion as a "moral cure" for criminals.

The point of greatest contact between the Christian churches and the penal system in the twentieth century was the prison chaplain. Ministers had always preached and conducted services in prisons, but in the twentieth century the chaplaincy evolved as a specific, separate program for bringing religion into the lives of prisoners. Not much specific information on the development and functioning of the prison chaplaincy is available. In general, it was conceived of as a means of providing religious services in prisons for believers, and as a means of converting non-believers to the Christian faith. Harry Elmer Barnes, a well-known criminologist, was highly critical of prison chaplains in his landmark *New Horizons in Criminology*, which first appeared in 1943.

> In the early days, the chaplain's success was usually measured by the number of conversions he was able to record. The wily inmate became adept in simulating religion for the purpose of gaining concessions or securing an early pardon. Some naive chaplains were all too eager to accept such outward expressions of religion as the genuine article. This made the chaplain appear ridiculous and lowered the effectiveness of the religious program within the institution.[53]

Barnes, true to the scientific spirit of the age, hints that the reason for chaplains' ineffectiveness is that they are not trained as social scientists. "It should be remembered that the chaplain's professional training is in the field of theology, rather than criminology or social work . . . The prison chaplaincy, while of some use to an enlightened criminology, is in need of adequate evaluation and increasingly realistic standards of preparation."[54]

With the arrival of the treatment model in the 1950's, a movement began toward "professionalization" of chaplains and improvement of chaplaincy services informed by disciplines such as sociology and psychology. The major religious faiths established chaplaincy associations to set standards and accredit prison chaplains. The chaplain would not simply provide religious services; nor would his task be isolated from the general goals of the treatment model. Rather, he would become part of the treatment staff of the prison. For instance, the Chaplain's Manual for one large urban prison system states:

> Through weekly religious services, repeated counsel, education, pastoral visiting and sacramental ministration, the chaplain helps the inmate establish a foundation in religious faith to support a continuing desire for self-improvement with ensuing benefit to the inmate and to society . . . the prison chaplain supplements and reinforces other professional treatment.[55]

In short, the role of religion is to assist in the "treatment" of offenders. Significantly, no conflict is recognized between the goals of the chaplain and the goals of the penal system. As the American Correctional Association's 1959 *Manual of Standards* expressed it: "It is felt . . . that the teaching of the church can be put into operation in any institution and need never impose upon the institutions a program in conflict with good

correctional management."[56] Just as Christian principles were invoked to sanctify earlier penal practices,
the proponents of treatment in prisons were careful to
incorporate chaplains into their model, so that once
again the legitimizing force of religion was employed in
support of the practices of American prisons.

Contemporary Penology

A 1975 study estimated there are approximately
400 prisons and some 5,200 jails.[57] Nor is there any
evidence, contrary to occasional optimistic predic-
tions of the media, that prisons are soon to be a thing
of the past. States and municipalities continue to build
such institutions and in 1975, the Federal Bureau of
Prisons requested $23.1 million for the construction of
new facilities.[58]

Jails are facilities run by municipal and county
governments. They are without a doubt the most frequently overlooked institutions in the criminal justice
system. Yet it is estimated that anywhere from half a
million to five million human beings are confined to
them in the course of a year,[59] and federal statistics
show that on an average day some 160,000 people are
being held in these institutions nation-wide.[60]

In theory, the modern jail is a place where individual defendants are held awaiting trial. But, as
Ronald Goldfarb pointed out in his study of jails: "The
jail has also come to be widely used both as a short-
term correctional institution for misdemeanants and a
way station for a random melange of other defendants."[61] In reality one finds a wide variety of people in
jails. Those convicted of serious offenses such as murder or rape may be incarcerated, awaiting transfer to a

state or federal facility or a trial on another charge. Offenders serving short sentences for minor offenses, e.g., ninety days for "disturbing the peace" are found in the jail. Jails also house "revolving-door offenders",[62] those individuals who are popularly considered socially undesirable or public nuisances, but have not been convicted of any serious crimes. Such offenders include alcoholics, narcotics addicts, prostitutes, vagrants, runaways and, until recently, homosexuals.

Despite the variety in the jail population, the human beings warehoused in a typical jail usually have something in common. In the words of Edith Flynn of the University of Illinois: "With few exceptions, the people (in jail) are poor, undereducated, unemployed and they belong to minority groups."[63] In short, people found in jail are the oppressed of American society. The economic deprivation of those in jail has been strikingly demonstrated. The 1970 National Jail Census conducted by the Law Enforcement Assistance Agency showed that 52% of those held in jails were defendants awaiting trial who could not afford bail.[64] Unconvicted, they were nonetheless imprisoned solely because they did not have sufficient funds to post bond. Likewise, a 1967 presidential task force on criminal justice found that in some states as many as 69% of those in local jails were there because they did not have the money to pay fines or meet alimony or support payments as directed by a court.[65]

As a rule, the physical facilities of jails are abysmal. Most jails were built many years ago, and suffer from either overcrowding, in the case of large urban jails, which hold over 50% of the national jail population, or from neglect, as in the case with many rural jails which see infrequent use and hence are not well-maintained. As Flynn summarized the problem: "The physical condition of most jails in this country is one of incipient decay . . . They are ill-equipped to meet even the most basic needs of their prisoners."[66]

There is no correctional program being implemented in American jails. In some of the larger urban systems, there are educational and treatment programs, designed to make jail life more productive and bearable. Some smaller jurisdictions have also developed programs for jail prisoners, usually to combat problems of drug abuse and alcoholism. In general, however, American jails are simply human warehouses. They are, in Ronald Goldfarb's description, "the ultimate ghetto".

Prisons, unlike their "poor relations", the jails, are intended to be the showcases of American penal practice. Run by the federal and state governments, they are as a rule more modern facilities than local jails and are better funded. Prisons are the institutions where convicted criminals are sent to serve their sentences, and where the business of "correction" or "punishment" or "treatment" is supposed to take place. On an average day some 200,000 human beings are confined to the federal and state prisons across the country. These people are the convicted felons—a term which ominously implies they must be the serious offenders or the proverbial "hardened criminals", until one learns that a felony is simply any crime which mandates a sentence over one year and a day.

On one level, it seems almost a matter of chance that certain individual criminals go to prison while others go free. For, out of every 100 felonies committed, only 1.5 ultimately result in imprisonment of the perpetrator.[67] Yet on another level, it is no accident that some criminals go to prison and others go free. For instance, black Americans are far more likely to be prosecuted for crimes and far more likely to ultimately be punished by imprisonment than are whites. Professor Donald Taft, writing in the 1950's, observed that:

> . . . Negroes are more likely to be suspected of crime than are whites. They are also more likely to be arrested. After arrest, Negroes are less likely to secure bail, and so are more liable to be counted in jail statistics. They are more liable than whites to be indicted and less likely to have their cases "nol prossed" or otherwise dismissed. If tried, Negroes are more likely to be convicted. If convicted, they are less likely to be given probation.[68]

Nor has the situation improved much since the publication of Taft's textbook. A 1973 study of Philadelphia courts revealed that "Blacks who plead guilty of a violent crime and are convicted are sent to jail in 64% of the cases compared to 42% of the cases for whites."[69] There is, likewise, a vast body of evidence to substantiate that the poor are more likely to be imprisoned than the rich, the well-known and influential are less likely to serve time in prison than the average age citizen, and so forth. Thus, as in the case of jails, to a large extent (although not exclusively), the human beings one finds in prisons are in some sense the oppressed of American society.

A good summary description of prisons is provided by the President's Commission of Law Enforcement and Administration of Justice:

Whatever the differences in type and quality among correctional institutions—there remains an inherent sameness about places where people are kept against their will.

It arises partly from restraint per se, whether symbolized by guns or by the myriad more subtle inhibitions on personal liberty. It arises from the isolation of the institutional community from the outside world and from the alienation and apartness of the inmate society. It is fed by the strangeness of living apart from families, with no choice about place of residence, selection of intimate associates, or type of occupation—all crucial values taken for granted in the outside world.[70]

In theory, it is in prisons that the modern "science of penology" is practiced. Yet, it is impossible to give a simple answer to the question: what model provides the basis for contemporary American prison practices? Perhaps the best is given by former Attorney General Ramsey Clark: "We cannot say that we practice any theory of penology in America today. We do what we do. And what we do has practically no relationship to what we say we do. Essentially we use penology—without saying so—to confine and thus separate for a time people who have committed crime. Simultaneously we punish by providing an unpleasant experience."[71]

In general, the American prison system is based on two conflicting models: one the remnant of the harsh and punitive descendants of the penitentiary; the other a remnant of the twentieth century movement toward treatment. As Donald Cressey expresses the dilemma:

Prison officials are supposed to be punitive. This is what prisons are all about, when it comes down to it . . . Inflicting pain is an unequivocal goal of prisons. The criminal law insists on it . . . Yet prison officials are also—in administering treatment—to be nonpunitive and non-restrictive . . . Because prisoners are to be changed, they are not to be punished . . . A warden who argues that his program is punitive and non-punitive must do some fast talking.[72]

Some of the more barbaric practices of American prisons have ceased—or at least become the exception and not the rule. Yet, since punishment is still a goal of the American penal system, to a large extent the evolution of penal practices has been "attempts to substitute psychological solitary confinement for the physical solitary confinement characterizing the early Pennsylvania and New York systems".[73] Prisoners are seldom physically abused, but they are nonetheless hurt and scarred. The carefully orchestrated regimen of the prison, including the supposedly humane treatment and rehabilitation programs, is a form of psychological and spiritual coercion and punishment. As Paul Keve, himself a professional working in corrections, admits:

Where he needs our assurance that he is a unique individual, our prisons proceed to discourage uniqueness in every way. He is given a haircut and a uniform like everyone else. He is put into a cell that duplicates hundreds of others, . . . He is deprived of decision-making opportunities . . . If we tried to design a regimen that would guarantee a reversal of everything which is needed to his help and correction, we could hardly do better than to resort to a conventional prison.[74]

Such evidence led the American Friends Service Committee, long active in attempts to reform prisons, to conclude in 1971 that: "Suffering within the penal system has not decreased. The opposite seems to be the case: rehabilitation has introduced a new form of brutality, more subtle and elusive."[75]

A popular misconception, promulgated by the media and political demagoguery, is that prisons have become essentially humane institutions, much like hospitals, where criminals have an easy existence. It is widely assumed that adequate chances for reformation via treatment and rehabilitation have been made available to prisoners, and that prisoners have exploited those chances. In reality, however, such chances have not been made available to prisoners, and instead treatment and rehabilitative ideals have been corrupted into means of psychological coercion. The problem is compounded by the vastly different perceptions of contemporary penal practices which are held by prison keepers and inmates. "Generally, the custodians are comfortably satisfied that they are good fellows doing the best they can to be fair under trying conditions and that if any inmate is dissatisfied with the process it only means that he does not fully realize what is best for him, or he, like the other prisoners, is always trying to beat the system anyway."[76] Inmates, on the other hand, tend to see members of the prison staff, particularly administrators and treatment personel, as hypocritical individuals of no greater virtue than themselves, and as having no particular interest in them other than to control their lives. This creates particular problems in terms of the prison's image with the public, for:

> When abuse becomes psychological instead of physical, when it is supplied by well-intentioned persons who do not intend to abuse, it is then in its worst form for it does not appear to the public as evil and so it is not made the subject of investigation and ameliorative effort. At the same time those prisoners who rebel against it have difficulty in articulating their complaints and the public is more certain of their unworthiness for having rebelled against an apparently benign administration.[77]

Today there is a growing tendency among Americans to call for a "hard line" or "get tough" stance on crime, which would only serve to make prisons harsher and more destructive institutions than they already are. As a system of crime control, then, American prisons are an incontestable failure. The National Advisory Commission on Criminal Justice Standards and Goals concluded in 1973:

> The failure of major institutions to reduce crime is incontestable. Recidivism rates are notoriously high. Institutions do succeed in punishing, but they do not deter. They protect the community, but that protection is only temporary. They relieve the community of responsibility by removing the offender, but they make successful reintegration into the community unlikely. They change the

committed offender, but the change is more likely to be negative than positive.[78]

As a system of human oppression and destruction, however, prisons are an unqualified success.

3
PRISONERS AS PEOPLE

To describe those in prisons as being (in general) minorities, the poor and the powerless, is not to say anything about them personally, as human beings. It is merely to describe their relative socio-economic status. The questions still remain: who does one find in prisons? What kind of people are they?

Despite the fact that few Americans have ever seen or been inside of a prison, let alone spent any appreciable amount of time with the people held captive there, most Americans have definite ideas about what kind of people convicted criminals are. However, they do not generally think of prisoners as human beings. Rather, they think of criminals as social types.[1] The criminal is an "animal", "inhuman monster", "sick", and all-around villain. All such "tags" on criminals serve to isolate and dehumanize them, and to prevent an understanding of them as people, "the human face of crime".

Popular stereotypes, however, are not the only source of information for most people's conceptions of crime. The terminology employed by treatment theorists to describe prisoners (e.g. "sub-marginal human beings"), leads some people, particularly college educated, middle-class liberals, to conceive of criminals as being sick individuals, who are incapable of free human action and are not responsible for their lives. It also influences some prisoners to conceive of

68

themselves in this way.[2] Likewise, countless studies of the "social organization of the prison" lead some individuals to a conclusion that prisoners can be easily fit into certain categories, based on their "functional role" in prison life or their "personality type".

But individuals who have no extensive first-hand experience with "criminals" would be misled if they uncritically accepted either popular opinion, or the highly acclaimed "scientifically objective" portraits of prisoners which are supposedly accurate reflections of the reality of prisons. For, as Dr. Milton Burglass accurately warns:

> Despite nearly 200 years of organized research into the question of crime, no one can today claim validated knowledge of the specific causes of criminal behavior or of a consistently effective means for its prevention. Every major 19th and 20th century theory of man, his psychology, his sociology, or his biology seems to have had its day in one form or another.[3]

History has seen much ideology and theory which tries to solve the problem of crime—which labels, categorizes and seemingly tries to "vanquish" criminals by explaining them away. It has seen little evidence of genuine human understanding.

In answering the question, "What kind of people does one find in prison", it will not do to simply rely upon conventional wisdom. Nor is it sufficient to quote statistics and studies, or to describe prisoners using the various labels which have been devised for them through the ages. It is necessary to attempt to portray the human side of prisoners—the experiences which most have been through, the perceptions which many of them share, ways in which prisons affect them, etc.

The following section is intended to give readers who have had no experiences with prisoners some idea of who they are, as people. For information, it relies upon those criminologists who have focused on the human experiences of criminals, and on the author's personal perceptions based upon extensive experiences in the criminal justice system.

The Prisoners–Recurring Life Themes

The "typical" inmate simply doesn't exist. Any statement one can make is necessarily a generalization with limited applicability in any individual case. When the complexity of even one individual's personality and the uniqueness of a single human life is taken into account, generalizations are of even more dubious value. Nonetheless, generalization is the only means by which it is possible to discuss any more than a single individual at one time, and therefore must suffice.

For practical reasons two "types" of inmates are not considered here. First, those few inmates who have been officially diagnosed and by all accounts are considered to be criminally insane have been excluded. Contrary to popular belief, and regardless of what treatment theorists claim, few residents of correctional institutions meet any recognized definition of mental illness, and the percentage of mentally ill inmates is no greater than that in the society at large.[4] Second, this chapter will not focus upon "situational" offenders, those whose crime was a desperate response to a highly unusual situation in an otherwise "conventional" life. (For example, the factory worker who begins to cash bad checks after his wife gets cancer.)

This leaves the vast majority of inmates for consideration: the so-called "traditional criminals". As noted above, there is no simple description for this group.

> Traditional criminals may operate singly or in groups; may be of high or low intelligence; may be occasional, habitual or compulsive; their crimes may be petty or highly dangerous; may involve violence or not . . . Some traditional criminals are steadily employed at legitimate work, some casual workers and still others rarely engage in legally gainful employment. In short, this is a diverse group of individuals.[5]

In trying to present some overall picture of those who end up in prison, a convenient initial observation lies in the fact that people in prison are, by definition, unsuccessful criminals. As Bruce Jackson notes:

> (Those in prison) represent the population that gets itself caught. With rare exceptions people do not go to jail just because they are guilty of something; they go to jail because they are too dumb or broke or clumsy to stay out.[6]

Considering the miniscule chances of one's actually serving time for having committed a crime, (less than two chances in a hundred), the very fact that a person is serving time in prison makes a statement about him or her. When the volume of crime in America as measured by numbers and dollars is considered, it becomes clear that those in prison represent a very special breed within their "profession": the losers. Or from another perspective, assuming the existence of a national "crime wave" or "crisis in law and order" in America, frequently the people one encounters in prison are not a large factor in maintaining it.

Chances are that for most prisoners the experience of failure is not limited to his/her criminal career, the proverbial "mistake" in an otherwise smooth life. On the contrary, in the case of many if not most people in prison, being incarcerated is simply the most recent crisis in a lifetime of difficult situations. Dr. Milton Burglass, himself a former inmate, and founder of the Thresholds program (a humanistic counseling program for prisoners currently operative nationwide) has observed:

> Commonly, one can note difficulties in the following areas:
> ——school: dropping out, adjustment problems, wide gap between functional and educational level;
> ——family: early and/or frequent conflicts in family, one or more broken marriages, illegitimate and abandoned children;
> ——job: failure to acquire job skills, instability, high frequency of conflict related job loss, etc.[7]

Some comment on these observations is in order. With respect to education, there is a popular belief concerning the mental deficiency of criminals.

Stereotypical portraits of the ignorant "con" lead to a conclusion that prisoners will be below average in intelligence and incapable of successfully undertaking any activity which requires intellectual ability. Evidence and experience belie this claim. Most studies indicate that intelligence scales in prisons overall are only slightly below normal.[8] Moreover while many inmates may lack in formal educational background and in skills measured by standard tests, they often develop keen intuition based on their substantial life experience. There is much to be said for the "wisdom of the streets". On a lesser but still widespread scale many inmates express interest in a wide range of subjects, most notably philosophy, politics and literature.[9] The individuals one finds in prison are not crippled by a lack of intellectual ability, but have an educational history marred by failure to cope with the educational system.

Interestingly one often finds painters, sculptors, poets, etc. in the prison population. Many inmates are highly sensitive to many different aspects of life experience and reflect that sensitivity in works of art. At times it seems that prisoners are more in touch with the basic rhythms of life than are most people because prisoners do not have the traditional social shields of education, money or social standing behind which to hide.

With respect to family, it is impossible to say just how many prisoners grew up in broken homes. The percentage is probably much lower than is commonly believed. Frequently prisoners had parents who cared, but couldn't cope. Yet even those inmates who once had relatively stable family relationships have likely had them shaken by frequent contact with the criminal justice system. People in prison who did not have strong family ties often developed surrogates for them. Gangs, for instance, sometimes supply emotional ties and support, and a sense of "belonging" or "having a place". Prisoners who were substantially raised in state institutions, such as orphanages or reform schools, often developed similar ties.

Prisoners are usually depicted as "cold-blooded" or heartless. It is assumed that criminals are destructive because they are devoid of emotion. As a rule, this is false. On the contrary, most people in prisons feel things very deeply. It is the very *intensity* of their relationships which often overwhelms them, leading them in turn to lash out at people and things around them.[10] Consider for instance a prisoner whose only loving relationship was with his grandmother, and who as a result threatens to kill his family when they have her committed to a distant retirement home; or the woman whose need for her "man" is so great that she would become a prostitute in order to support his drug habit; or the gang member whose loyalty is so blind that he viciously assaults a rival gang member in front of the police, simply because the rival punched a fellow member of his gang. People in prison are impulsive perhaps, but by no means is it accurate to portray them as heartless.

On the other hand, street relationships, which are a large part of many prisoners' lives, tend to be superficial, unstable and influenced by the survival ethic. Based on his years in interviewing prisoners, Jackson describes street life:

You hustle for a living and everyone hustles you. The cops shake you down, the lawyers take what

the cops didn't get, the women expect the money
to be there and the hell with you if you're not
bringing it in. In this world, precious little is done
for love.

Relationships are usually transitory, epidem-
eral and conditional.[11]

It would be wrong to conclude that people in
prison are incapable of establishing warm, human relationships with others or are so jaded as to completely
reject the overtures of others, as the "hardened criminal" myth would suppose. Still, it is equally important
to recognize some of the harsher realities experienced
by many people in prison. As noted above, the extent
to which these experiences are real varies from individual to individual. A number of inmates, most notably those in the "professional thief" mode described
by Edward Sutherland's classic study, seem to have a
high degree of calculation in their acts and organization in their lives, and to them the above description
would be less applicable.[12] But as John Irwin (among
others) has observed, "the bulk of convicted felons,
'disorganized criminals', pursue a chaotic, purposeless
life, filled with unskilled, careless and variegated criminal activity".[13] Most drug and alcohol related offenses
would be included in this grouping.

One notable theme in most prisoners' lives is a
combination belief in fatalism/determinism which affects their outlook in every situation. Considering their
life history of chronic failure in a number of areas,
including crime, people in prison come to view themselves as incapable of having an effect upon events in
their lives. This phenomenon has been observed by a
number of authors, and is best described by Grahm

Sykes as a "billiard ball" conception of reality, where one is helplessly propelled from one situation to another.[14] This dovetails with a tone of self-defeatism, a "what's the use" attitude which assumes that since the individual has failed to influence events in the way he/she desired in the past, it is impossible for him/her to do so in the present. This in turn translates into a negative self-image whereby prisoners see themselves as losers. It is no accident that the phrase "born to lose" is often tattooed on some part of an inmate's body.[15]

The implication contained in this world view is that an individual is not accountable for what happens to him/her or what he/she does:

> . . . bad luck is an extenuating condition and thus a defense to crime. A man's fortune is not his fault. Since a man is not responsible for his fortune, he cannot be responsible for its unfolding.[16]

Generally prisoners (unlike treatment theorists) recognize, however, that determinism in its many forms cannot realistically be advanced as the explanation of everything, and so they oscillate back and forth between seeing themselves as free or determined, depending upon the situation in which they find themselves.[17]

A related theme in many prisoners' understanding of their world is the survival ethic. In one inmate's words:

> There are really only two classes of people—marks and con men. I didn't make the rules, I just live by them.

You know how it is in this dog-eat-dog world.
You got to take the other guy before he takes you.
You know, the real sharpies out with the marks.
Of course it depends on how you get ahead. My
way was no different from a lawyer or a business
man. You know a lawyer has a license to steal.[18]

In short, the individual is seen as being thrown
into a harsh uncaring world, where he/she is forced
into a vicious competition for survival. One may not
necessarily care for the life he/she leads, but there is
no choice in the matter. It should be emphasized that
for many inmates, in view of their struggle in "getting
over" from day-to-day, this is not by any means an
unrealistic or illusionary conception of life.

A final theme critical to any understanding of
most prisoners' perception of the world is the "sense
of injustice", a term first coined by legal philosopher
Edmond Cahn in his attempt to describe the mechanics
of law and justice.[19] This concept, or its equivalent,
was later incorporated into the analyses of many
criminologists relative to an understanding of convicts:

Adult criminals have felt some sense of injustice
for various reasons for many years. The feeling
stemmed first, from their perception of the inequality of social circumstances in which they were
born, grew up in, and competed as adults. Second, they perceived unfairness and inequality because of corruption and class bias in the way they
were handled by law enforcement agencies and
the courts . . .[20]

The significance of this sense of injustice is pointed out
by Grahm Sykes in his book *Crime and Society*:

Punishment must symbolize the ethical condemnation of *legitimate* society; for if this is lacking,
the police, courts and prisons are reduced to the
level of opponents instead of maintaining their position as dispensers of impartial justice.[21]

The prisoner then, perceiving the existence of unfairness and corruption in society, challenges society's
standing to condemn him/her:

I never did envy anybody that was a member of
society, frankly. I haven't a hell of a lot of use for
society. Not when I've been taking care of (paying
off) those members of your society, district attor-
neys and judges.[22]

The sense of injustice which exists among inmates
is all too frequently dismissed as a self-serving rationalization for criminal behavior. This view fails to
recognize that in fact many if not most inmates have
been treated unfairly by specific institutions in society,
particularly the judicial system, and do have substantial grounds for considering themselves to be oppressed. Given the existence of injustice, and the perception of it by prisoners, any arguments defending the
legitimacy of prisons and the right of society to punish
will carry little weight with those inside the prison.

The reality of a situation, however, is never quite
as simple or clear-cut as descriptions of it. Therefore,
having made a series of observations about whom one
finds in prison, for accuracy's sake, it is necessary to
refine them by further qualification. Thus, while it is
true that most inmates are highly critical of society and
its treatment of them, and condemn it for being unjust

and hypocritical, it does not follow that they completely reject society or conventional values:

> . . . the lawbreaker does not necessarily repudiate the imperatives of the dominant normative system, despite his failure to follow them. Instead, he may see himself caught up in a dilemma which must be resolved, unfortunately at the cost of breaking the law . . . (or) Deviation from certain norms may occur not because the norms are rejected but because other norms, held to be more pressing or involving a higher loyalty, are accorded precedence.[23]

This partial acceptance of social norms, translated into a partial acceptance of society's verdict against him, presents a critical problem for the inmate's self-understanding. As Sykes has observed:

> Now it is sometimes claimed that many criminals are so alienated from conforming society and so identified with a criminal subculture that moral condemnation, disapproval, or rejection by legitimate society do not touch them; they are, it is said, indifferent . . . at least as far as the moral stigma of being criminal is concerned. Possibly this is true for a small number of offenders . . . For the great majority of prisoners, however, the evidence suggests that neither alienation from the ranks of society nor involvement in a system of criminal values is sufficient to eliminate the threat to the prisoner's ego posed by society's rejection . . . The wall which seals off the criminal, the contaminated man, is a constant threat to the pris-

oner's self-conception and the threat is daily repeated in reminders that he must be kept apart from "decent" men.[24]

Looked at from another perspective, the "hardened criminal" stereotype of the amoral, antisocial, intractable deviant, is inaccurate. Sociologists Lloyd McCorkle and Richard Korn have suggested that one of the central problems for the prisoner is how he/she copes with the feeling of rejection by society. In their view, prisoners cope partially by "rejecting the rejectors".[25]

There unquestionably exists in the minds of most inmates feelings of doubt about themselves, remorse about their crimes, and guilt about their lives. Yet, since it is necessarily hidden beneath various defenses and justifications, it is often overlooked in portrayals of inmates. The fight for spiritual and psychological survival requires that prisoners avoid being vulnerable at all costs. They must always maintain a front to justify themselves and their lives whatever the doubts and fears they may harbor inside. As David Matza says, the criminal "excuses himself, but his gruff manner has obscured the fundamental sense in which he begs our pardon".[26] Or, in one prisoner's words: "Don't be fooled by me. Don't be fooled by the face I wear. Please hear what I'm not saying."[27]

The degrading conditions of the prisons themselves, and the often brutal practices used in maintaining them, are also recognized by prisoners as reflections of society's attitude towards them as human beings. Their protest against these conditions, however, serves as evidence that they are not irrevocably committed to a fatalistic/ deterministic outlook, but can and do break from that to assert themselves as well:

> Members of the Observers Committee during the
> Attica riots noticed "most of all the inmates stress
> again and again their desire for respect. 'We will
> be treated as human beings.' Another, near tears,
> swears 'we will live like people or die like men'."[28]

Therefore, any portrait of inmates which presents
them solely as determined creatures unwilling or incapable of free human action, is both incomplete and
demeaning. For along side of, and often in spite of,
their tragic experiences and fatalistic world view, prisoners are human beings who wish to live and be
treated with dignity.

In a study of this kind, it is only logical that some
attention be given to the religious views of prisoners.
Traditionally, religion within the prison has been concerned with prisoners' denominational affiliation, their
professed belief in God, their attendance at religious
services or classes, and whether or not prisoners were
"sincere" about "religion" based on their behavior in
the prison. On the whole, religion in the prison has
been identified with ritual-services, baptisms, the traditional manifestations of religious belief, and religios-
ity has been identified with pious behavior. Ministry
within the prison has been too concerned with convicts "getting religion", that is, being baptised and embracing the outward manifestations of religious belief.
Many inmates who seemingly reject religion, because
they have no time for the way it has commonly been
practiced in prison, are assumed to be non-religious
people. This overlooks the fact that many prisoners
have a personal history of religious training which con-

tributes greatly to their self-understanding and world view, and which also contributes to their understanding of such subjects as good and evil, freedom and responsibility, punishment and reward, justice, etc.

Most prisoners, like many other people, approach the subject of religion from two perspectives. A distinction can be drawn between prisoners' views of religion as it is represented by specific religious institutions, and their personal religious beliefs which are the product of reflection upon their own life experiences; although prisoners themselves seldom make this distinction in their own minds. On the contrary, when speaking about religion they tend to confuse the two and consequently often appear to be ambivalent in their feelings about God, the church and other related issues. All the same, this distinction, between prisoners' views on the cultural manifestations of religion, and religious topics in themselves, is crucial in understanding how prisoners understand religion.

In terms of the cultural manifestations of religion, most prisoners today are not *actively* affiliated with an organized church. In large part, this is because prisoners have experienced religious institutions as hypocritical, and either unable or unwilling to respond to the needs of their community. Most prisoners have not witnessed individual Christians or Christian institutions as living the Gospel they preach, and therefore have had little reason to believe that anyone is a better person for professing any particular religious faith. As one prisoner expressed it: "Convicts have a low opinion of most Christians . . . as hypocritical, once-a-week devotees who scramble for money, caring little for their fellow man and spouting moral platitudes which they can hide behind but don't live up to."[29]

Frequently, prisoners have come to view clergy as authority figures, who work to perpetuate unjust societal institutions and maintain the status quo. At the same time they have often experienced clergy as individuals who are quick to judge their lives and condemn them for wrongdoing, while ignoring the widespread injustice in society which many prisoners view as the cause of their being in jail. In institutions where the chaplain is considered to be a member of the institutional staff, inmates may be slow to trust them for fear that their confidences will be betrayed to members of the treatment or custody staff.[30]

Many prisoners seem to have been exposed to orthodox or fundamentalist ideas about Christianity as they grew up. They are critical of the harshness of fundamentalism, and are also critical of the "pie-in-the-sky" attitudes which simplistic orthodoxy often leads to. To many prisoners, based on their experience, belief in God and churchgoing is foolish idealism, irrelevant to them in trying to cope with experiences in "the real world". Even prisoners who do attend services are not necessarily ready to embrace religious beliefs. As one chaplain observed:

We, as chaplains, know very well that only about 25 per cent of the prisoners attend our Chapel Service with any real sincerity. We know too, that of those who do attend, religion may or may not be the inducing factor. Many men merely attend to get out of their cells, some go to hear the music, quite a few feel that Chapel attendance may influence the Parole Board in their favor. Others go because relatives and friends urge them to. With many, attendance is nothing more than a

superstitious habit with no comprehension of the
real significance of religion.[31]

At the same time that prisoners are indifferent to
organized religion, however, and are "highly critical of
those who profess spiritual and moral values",[32] very
few prisoners seem to deny the existence of God, and a
surprising number of them seem to view their imprisonment as a sign of God's judgment against themselves. They reflect a fundamental notion of God as
being intimately connected in the affairs of every-
day life. One study of institutionalized delinquents,
conducted by the American Baptists Convention, dis-
covered that they had "very elemental religious beliefs
and related their life experience to direct causes of a
pleased or displeased Omnipotence. They saw God
much as a good and loving father figure or a tyrannical,
unjust despot".[33] Chaplains often remark that many of
the prisoners with whom they come into contact feel
that the sentence which the judge imposed upon them
is reflective of God's displeasure with their lives.
    In view of such beliefs, and of the sense of guilt
which affects convicts generally, it should not be surprising that many prisoners have a feeling that they are
condemned without hope. This is not necessarily reflected in a strong acceptance of the religious myth of
Hell, but more in a general feeling that their lives are
beyond hope, and that whatever validity there may be
to religious belief, it cannot help them because their
lives will never change. While prisoners are not apt to
speak of this sense of unworthiness, and certainly are
not likely to speak of it in traditional religious terms,
such as sinfulness, many feel that evil is present in
their lives, and the most fundamentalist prisoners will

even resort to the explanation: "the devil made me do it".

In short, when many prisoners reflect on religion in terms of their own personal experience, it is reflection rooted in despair. Perhaps that is why so many inmates appear loathe to speak about religion, or even hostile to those who wish to do so. For large numbers of prisoners, religion is a profoundly negative experience, something which is frequently nothing other than apparent silliness, or else something frightening beyond description.

4
PENAL IDEOLOGY VS.
CHRISTIAN BELIEF

Aside from the specific models and practices of the American penal system there are a number of general penal theories which provide rationales and explanations for the punishment of criminals. In general, penal theorists defend imprisonment on the grounds of retribution, deterrence, and treatment. Virtually all penal theory begins and ends with the premise that punishment of criminals must take place. Thus, what penal theory really involves is the defense and promotion of the existing institutions of punishment—the state, the criminal law, the prisons. For that reason, it is really more accurate to describe penal "theory" as ideology. This ideological bias is reflected in the fact that there is little debate among penal theorists over whether we *should* or should not punish. The central controversy is always: *on what grounds* should we punish?

Larger issues loom behind the debates of penal ideologists. Ultimately, all of them are concerned with the question posed by Russian author Leo Tolstoy: "By what right do some people punish others?" As legal philosopher H.L.A. Hart warned:

> . . . the major positions concerning punishment, which are called retributive or deterrent or refor-

mative "theories" of punishment are moral *claims* as to what justifies the practice of punishment— claims as to why, morally, it *should* or *may* be used.[1]

The first task confronting us as Christians is to face the moral issues raised by penal ideology, and then to discard it as an acceptable framework for approaching the problem of crime.

    The issues raised by penal ideology are not necessarily ethical questions for the Christian. More fundamentally, they are questions of belief: what do I understand my Christianity to mean, and how in turn does this understanding influence the way in which I face the reality of crime? It is only by first considering these two belief questions that an ethical challenge is presented to the Christian: given my understanding of Christianity, and its world view, to what extent is that outlook consistent with, or opposed to, penal ideology?

The Inadequacy of Retribution

    Generally stated, the key principle of retribution contends that: those who "do evil" *deserve* to suffer as a matter of right or justice. The popular sentiment "he had it coming to him" is a reflection of the concept of retribution. The notion that one must pay for misdeeds is also an offspring of retribution theory. Two particular concepts of retribution will be considered here: 1) retribution as an institutionalized, legitimized (and even sanctified) form of vengeance against wrongdoers; and 2) retribution as a reflection of a particular philosophical or theological understanding of existence. Any critique of retribution is complicated because Christianity became entangled with the idea in the course of its evolution. Therefore in this section the focus is as much Christian theology and its uses, as it is penal ideology *per se*.

The first, and by far the most popular understanding of retribution is that of righteous vengeance for crimes committed. The Old Testament concept of *lex talionis*, the law of retaliation, "an eye for an eye, a tooth for a tooth, . . . a life for a life" is interpreted literally as being a command of God and/or "Justice". The concept of "lex talionis" frequently turns up in penal literature and even more frequently in the thinking of the American public. In contemporary America, there are "neo-Puritans" who take the biblical injunction no less seriously than their ancestors and vehemently insist that righteousness demands strict retaliation against criminals.

Not surprisingly, the concept of retaliation receives religious justification because of its inclusion in the bible. Karl Menninger cites a clergyman's syndicated column calling for vengeance as the Christian way to deal with criminals.[2] Evangelist-preacher, Billy Graham's famous remark that rapists ought to be castrated is a perfect example of this type of thinking.

The widespread application of the biblical law of retaliation to contemporary criminal justice, and the general tendency to read the Old Testament as a book about God's righteous and vindicative judgment against sinful humanity which corresponds to it, reflects a poor understanding of theology, and is *the* classic example of the misuse of a theological concept to legitimize and rationalize human penal practice. Theologically, the major problem with the use of the *lex talionis* as a divine endorsement of retaliation against criminals is that it is a completely mistaken interpretation of the text. According to Scripture scholars, the Old Testament prescription "an eye for an eye, a tooth for a tooth" was not a divine imperative or command. Rather, it was a limit upon human vengeance.[3] The purpose of it was to restrict retaliation for crime and thereby avoid an escalating spiral of violence as a result of blood feuds between clans. The *lex talionis* meant no *more* than an eye could be taken in retaliation for the loss of an eye, no *more* than one life could be taken in retaliation for murder, etc. Its purpose was to ensure some sense of proportionality between crime and punishment. To interpret the *lex* as a divine imperative is simply wrong.

Literal interpretation of the *lex talionis* is symptomatic of a wider tendency to interpret all of the Old Testament as being representative of a God whose essential attribute is justice and who insists on vindictive punishment of wrongdoers. Such an understanding of the Old Testament again rests upon questionable scriptural judgment. For within the Old Testament itself, strict retaliation did not prevail. As Raymond de Vaux observed:

> In the oldest text, that of Exodus, it (the lex talionis) is in fact followed immediately by a law which orders the liberation of a slave in compensation for the loss of an eye or a tooth (Ex. 21:26-27), and it is preceded by a law which, for an injury inflicted in a fight, orders only the payment of a compensation and medical expenses (Ex. 21:18-19). Only in one case is strict retaliation exacted: the guilty murderer must die and cannot buy his freedom. This rigour is justified by a reli-

gious reason: the blood which has been shed has profaned the land in which Yahweh dwells (Nb. 35:31-34).[4]

As Vaux goes on to point out, the Israelite code compared quite favorably with other early Eastern codes in terms of being humane. Flogging, for example, could not exceed forty strokes, "lest the bruises be dangerous and your brother be degraded". (Deut. 25:3) And the Israelite code, "unlike other Eastern laws, limited capital punishment to offences against the purity of worship, against the sanctity of life and the sources of life, and this religious motive is usually expressed in the laws".[5]

This last point concerning the religious character of Israelite society and law is crucial. Israel was a theocracy. As Emil Brunner described it:

The law of the state was at the same time the law of the religious community and the law of the religious community was the law of the state. The laws of religion and the synagogue were enforced by the same coercive means as those of the state, and transgressions of them punished in the same way as transgression of civic law.[6]

When the Old Testament speaks of law, justice and punishment, it does so in light of the Hebrews' self-understanding as a people of God. Law was not considered a man-made institution, nor was it seen as a burden or a limit on the people. It was the gift of Yahweh, His direction in leading the people to Himself. Justice, literally translated, was "righteousness". It did not have the modern connotation of a balancing between good and evil. It referred to the right or proper relationship between God and his people, and between individual members of the community, as revealed by Yahweh. Israel, therefore, cannot simplistically be conceived of as a political entity similar to the modern state. Israel was a nation, but it was also a cult. To generalize on the basis of the Old Testament, to take standards specifically applicable to the Israelite experience and to apply them uncritically to modern reality, is totally absurd. To attempt such a transfer, as some penal theorists and many Christians are wont to do, is, in Brunner's analogy, "as devastating in its effects as a transfusion of blood between different blood groups. Healthy blood so transfused is fatal".[7]

A final theological problem stemming from such literal biblical exegis is that it misunderstands the general function of punishment in the Old Testament. A common error is to regard the God of the Old Testament as one who punishes for the sake of vengeance, as a wrathful God who is satiated by punishment, much in the same way that pagan gods were believed to have been satisfied by blood sacrifices. Such a conception of the function of the Old Testament punishment overlooks the fact that the basic purpose of Yahweh's judgment and subsequent punishment was to turn the Israelites away from their sinfulness and back to the path of righteousness, which led to life in communion (covenant) with Yahweh. Yahweh's judgment and punishment were never final, as they would have been had punishment essentially been retributive in nature. The healing nature of punishment was embodied in the covenant with David. As John Sheehan puts it: "When David errs, God will assuredly punish him . . . But he will punish him 'as a father punishes a son'. The Davidic covenant was unconditioned. No matter what happened, no matter how sorely Israel sinned, the Lord would never abandon her . . ."[8] This notion is best summarized, (although by no means wholly contained in) the prophet Ezekiel's later writings where it is written:

> As I live, says the Lord God, I swear I take no pleasure in the death of the wicked man, but rather in the wicked man's conversion, that he may live. Turn, turn from your evil ways! Why should you die, O house of Israel? (Ex. 33:10)

In sum, it would seem to be a straightforward conclusion that any kind of a "neo-Puritan", literal reading and interpretation of the bible as a justification for retributive punishment (understood as retaliation) is unacceptable.

Retribution theory in its other forms, however, is far more sophisticated. One famous modern defender was Pope Pius XII. Pius' defense of retribution is treated here in some detail, because it is frequently cited as a religious endorsement of retribution and because it is a representative presentation of much Christian thought on the subject.[9] Before considering the defense, however, it is first necessary to understand the Roman Church's historical position on punishment as it was expressed in the Canon Law, for Pius builds upon this foundation in advancing his arguments.

Punishment in the Canon Law was classified according to three purposes.[10] First, there were censures, which were referred to as "medicinal penalties" (canon 2241), the purpose of which was to correct offenders and turn them away from evil and back to the good. Next, there was vindictive penalties (c. 2286), the purpose of which was satisfaction for crime and expiation for it, regardless of the correction of the offender. And, finally, there were penal remedies (c. 2306) and penances (c. 2312), which warned offenders and also allowed them to avoid other, harsher penalties. In general, however, the Catholic tradition centered on the dual function of punishment as being both medicinal (i.e. corrective, healing) and vindictive (i.e. giving satisfaction and expiation for crime). In his most important speech, Pius combined the vindictive and medicinal aspects of punishment, and argued that punishment of criminals was justified because it served the purpose of "righting and restoring disturbed harmony" while at the same time "such punishment can and should help toward his definitive rehabilitation, provided man himself does not raise barriers to its efficacy".[11]

With respect to the vindictive (retributive) function of punishment, Pius argues that:

> . . . the order violated by the criminal act demands the restoration and re-establishment of the equilibrium which has been disturbed. It is the proper task of law to guard and preserve the harmony between duty, on the one hand, and law, on the other, and to re-establish this harmony if it has been injured . . . This order of duty is necessarily an expression of the order of being, of the order of the true and the good, which alone has their right of existence, in opposition to error and evil, which represent that which should not exist.[12]

Pius maintains that punishment effectively restores the order violated by crime because it compels the criminal to suffer, by imposing an evil upon him/her. The suffering of the criminal, however, is not necessarily damaging to him/her. Rather, Pius says, "To suffer in this life means practically a turning of the soul within itself; it is a path which drives one from the superficial to deep within oneself. Considered in that light, suffering has great moral value."[13] Punishment therefore, is "a source of interior purification on this earth", and therefore has a "religious and holy meaning".[14] Thus, in suffering vindictive punishment for his/her acts, the criminal is healed and purified. Retribution and reformation are not contradictory; they become complementary. Should punishment and suffering not be a healing experience, Pius maintains, it is because the criminal refuses to allow himself or herself to be open to its medicinal effects.

To anyone even remotely familiar with the problems of criminal justice, Pius' defense of retribution has an air of unreality about it. His idealistic conceptions of the penal system are totally inconsistent with the reality of punishment. For punishment by imprisonment reforms precious few individuals. On the contrary, it brutalizes, de-humanizes and embitters the majority of those who experience it. Imprisonment does not cleanse or purify human beings—it corrupts them. But to dismiss Pius' theory solely on the grounds that it does not seem to accurately reflect the reality of the situation is to miss the much larger problem which it represents. Pius' approach to theology is typical of a perennial tendency of Christians to focus attention not on the world, and the presence of God within the world, but to concentrate on heavenly visions or intellectual abstractions apart from the world.

As a result, theological language tends toward meaninglessness, and people seek explanations for the world and guidance in approaching it from other sources.

With Pius (as with so much Christian theology), the problem stems specifically from his reliance upon Greek philosophy in trying to understand the problem of justice and the mystery of human beings. For there is an indisputable clash between the classical Greek and the biblical perspective on life in the world. Where Socrates welcomes death, Jesus rejects and fears it.[15] To the Greek philosophers life in the world is but a shadow of the world. To the Jew and the Christian, human history holds a place of central importance and Christians must necessarily take the world seriously.

This is no idle, academic distinction, but has great significance for the way in which we as Christians approach the problem of crime and punishment. Pius, in approaching them, embraced what was an essentially Greek concept of justice, that of equilibrium, of harmony. Such an understanding of justice is far removed from the original biblical conception of it.

> Greece had only one thing lacking in the circle of her moral and intellectual activity, but this was an important void . . . Her philosophers, while dreaming of the immortality of the soul, were tolerant towards the iniquities of this world . . . Israel never stood quietly by to see the world so badly governed under the authority of a God reputed to be just. Her sage burnt with anger over the abuses of the world . . . The Israelitish prophets were impetuous writers such as we of the present day should denounce as anarchists and socialists.

They were fanatics in the cause of social justice
and loudly proclaimed that if the world were not
just, or capable of becoming so, it had better be
destroyed . . .[16]

Based on the Greek mode of thought, we have wrongly
divided the concept of justice into two parts: distributive justice, referring to the general allocating of resources and benefits in a society (i.e. social justice);
and retributive justice, which involves the preservation of the "eternal equilibrium" or "proper order" of
existence (i.e. criminal justice). Such a distinction, totally alien to biblical thought, allows us to zealously
pursue the punishment of criminals (retribution), while
ignoring the larger social inequities (distribution)
which, in most cases, are the ultimate cause of crime.
"While the Greek philosophers were probing into the
nature of virtue, the Hebrew prophets were decrying
the vice of moral evil precipitated by the natural inequality of man caused by his differences in intellectual, physical and material endowment, which
became the source of unruly power."[17] The real problem with Pius' defense of retribution is that he repeats
this error; he attempts to focus exclusively on the
problem of "paying back" criminals in isolation from
the larger and more significant social injustices which
breed crime and permeate the criminal justice system.
    Once again, the distinction is not an idle one, be-
cause on one point, Pius was certainly correct:
punishment will never have a salutary effect upon
criminals until they view it as being justly incurred.
This point was echoed by British writer Toby Jackson:

Offenders who regard punishment as a deserved

deprivation resulting from their own misbehavior are qualitatively different from offenders who regard punishment as a misfortune bearing no relationship to morality. Thus, a child who is spanked by his father and the member of a . . . gang who is jailed for carrying concealed weapons are both "punished". But one accepts the deprivation as legitimate and the other bows before superior force . . . punishment has rehabilitative significance only for the former.[18]

Recalling the sense of injustice which permeates the outlook of most people in prison today, one is forced to conclude that "rehabilitation" cannot take place there. Prisoners do not, as a rule, view their punishment as just or well-intentioned. They reason that even if they deserve punishment, they certainly do not deserve to suffer the inhumanity of imprisonment. While in some cases this "sense of injustice" is largely a rationalization for criminal acts, in the majority of cases it stems from having actually been a victim of injustice and social oppression. As Karl Menninger accurately observed in his book, appropriately titled *The Crime of Punishment*, prisoners, coming from the poor and socially unpopular, are as much sinned against as they are sinners.[19] If we wish to speak of justice in any meaningful way, we must include in the scope of justice "crimes against criminals". Until we re-discover the original all-encompassing meaning of the biblical conception of justice, and overcome the false dichotomy between its "retributive" and "distributive" aspects, it is perfectly meaningless to speak of punishment as being in any way purifying or reformatory, because prisoners will refuse to see their punishment as just and will instead (often) view it as simply another form of oppression against them, taken by an already repressive society.

Retribution theory was not quite so prominent in the Protestant theology as it was in Catholic thought. Punishment was not conceived of so much in terms of desert, as it was in terms of the application of necessary force by God's minister in the world, the state. Still, retribution theory did find its way into some Protestant theology.[20]

A representative Protestant view of retribution is provided in the writing of Emil Brunner:

> All earthly criminal justice is based on the presumption of a divine, holy order which must not be infringed, and the infringement of which requires restitution, atonement, punishment. Properly understood, the human judge is merely a representative of God. He acts in the name of the divinely established order of the community . . . It is precisely the sword, the punishment of death, which should be the expression of God's holy wrath at the infringement of the divine order.[21]

The most significant flaw with such a model, its identification of the state as a minister of God, based on a highly literal interpretation of some portions of the New Testament, will be dealt with later. In addition to that weakness, it shares the Catholic preoccupation with the abstract, as opposed to the human aspects of justice. Likewise, it fails to fully appreciate the unitary quality of the concept of justice as it was expressed in the bible. Finally, it suffers from the same misinterpretation of scripture, both Old Testament and New Testament, as discussed above, whereby God is viewed primarily as one who is wrathful and indignant over the sinful acts of human beings.

A number of New Testament passages bear directly upon the questions of retaliation and retribution. With respect to the *lex talionis*, it is explicitly repudiated by Jesus. "You have heard that it was said, 'an eye for an eye, and a tooth for a tooth'. But now I tell you: do not take revenge on someone who does you wrong." (Matt. 5:38-39) Traditionally this passage, and the Sermon on the Mount in general, have been dismissed as not applying to the social realm. Yet this is a tenuous assumption at best. For in the Pentateuch and the Talmud there is no separate term for ethics as opposed to law.[22] Law and ethics, the public and the private, were inseparable. It is only a modern, post-Reformation way of thinking which allows us to make a division between the public and private spheres of morality. At the same time, responsibility for the enforcement of the law lay with the individual members of the community. The degree to which the law was strictly or loosely enforced depended directly upon the will of the members of the community. When someone witnessed a crime, or had a crime committed against them, the decision to bring the fact to light and appeal to the law was in many cases a personal decision. The modern notion of crime as being a "breach of the King's peace" or a "threat to the state" was alien. There was nothing like the contemporary, institutionalized criminal justice system. Law was intimately connected with the life of the community. Thus Jesus' rejection of the "lex talionis" would most certainly have an effect on the life of the community as a whole, not just in the private lives of individual members of it. We display a characteristic modern bias in assuming automatically that what Jesus had to say has no application beyond a purely personal sphere.[23]

In place of vengeance, Jesus substituted an ethic of love. "You have heard it said, 'Love your friends, hate your enemies'. But now I tell you: love your enemies, and pray for those who persecute you". (Matt. 5:43-44) As part of that ethic, he rejected the condemnation of others: "Do not judge others, and God will not judge you; do not condemn others, and God will not condemn you; forgive others, and God will forgive you." (Luke 6:37)

In his teaching on judging others, Jesus emphasized that finding fault with others was a convenient means of avoiding criticism of self.

Why do you look at the speck in your brother's eye, but pay no attention to the log in your own? How can you say to your brother, 'Please, brother, let me take that speck out of your eye', yet not even see the log in your own eye? You hypocrite! Take the log out of your own eye first, and then you will be able to see and take the speck out of your brother's eye. (Luke 6:41-42)

The validity of this insight is certainly apparent in terms of the modern tendency to separate social (distributive) from criminal (retributive) justice. As a society we fail to see the inequality and economic deprivation which is ultimately at the root of crime. Yet at the same time we insist on harsh punishments for isolated, individual acts. As a result, our criminal justice system is neither just nor effective in reforming criminals, for prisoners readily recognize the hypocrisy of it all.

"One blind man cannot lead another one; if he does, both will fall into a ditch." (Luke 6:39)

All of retribution theory is built upon the concept of desert. Unless it is valid to think in terms of rewarding or punishing human beings on the basis of what they supposedly deserve, retribution theory is baseless. Christian support of retribution theory is ultimately rooted in a conception of God as Judge—one who will at the end of time give unto each according to his/her due. Yet, such a belief is based on what is at best a very selective reading of the New Testament, because in many places the concept of desert is violated. Perhaps the most explicit rejection of desert is the parable of the laborers in the vineyard (Matt. 20:1-16). In the parable, the master of the vineyard hires workers throughout the day. Some work a full day in the hot sun. Others, hired later, work only an hour in the coolness of afternoon. Yet all are paid the same wage, a certain "injustice" if one accepts the concept of desert. In another instance, Jesus criticizes those who would seek reward for their actions, and notes that God "makes his sun to shine on good and bad people alike, and gives rain to those who do good and those who do evil". (Matt. 5:45) Or, in Luke, Jesus teaches that followers who have completely fulfilled their duty should still consider themselves to be "unprofitable servants". (Luke 17:10) Finally, even if it is proper for God to judge, it by no means follows that human beings should presume to exercise God's prerogative for him. This was Paul's teaching to the Romans:

If someone does evil to you, do not pay him back with evil. Try to do what all men consider to be good. Do everything possible on your part, to live at peace with all men. Never take revenge, my friends, but instead let God's wrath do it. For the Scripture says, "I will take revenge, I will pay back, says the Lord." Instead, as the scripture says: "if he is thirsty, give him a drink; for by doing this you will heap burning coals on his head." Do not let evil defeat you; instead, conquer evil with good.

It was only when the Church mistakenly came to understand itself as the Kingdom on earth that the notion of human punishment with divine sanction grew and flourished. Modern Christianity has outgrown the tendency to view itself as the earthly representative of the divine order. It remains for Christian retributive theology and the penal ideology to which it gave rise to do likewise. From these and other passages it is clear that the principle of desert is by no means sanctified in the New Testament. If anything, it is challenged.

No argument is being advanced here that the prescriptions of Jesus can be literally transferred from the New Testament and applied to modern times as a social agenda. To attempt to do so would be as absurd as the attempts to transplant Old Testament law, which were criticized earlier. Certainly there are significant problems with applying New Testament teaching to the harsh realities of modern life, which will be considered in later chapters. On the other hand, Christians are all too quick to dismiss the relevance of what Jesus taught for social situations, and refuse to consult scripture for motivating principles and standards. And ignorance of scriptural revelation can ultimately prove fatal to Christian belief.

Aside from the dubious biblical basis for the idea of retribution, building Christian theology on a retributive foundation leads to a significant problem. The problem stems from the fact that intuitively there seems to be little virtue in undertaking any activity simply to avoid punishment or to seek a reward. Yet, in the final analysis, retributive theory is based on just such a conception of morality.

Historically, Christianity in popular preaching has centered upon the goal of attaining eternal life in heaven and avoiding the fires of hell. Belief in God, and love of God, were largely means to an end, i.e. personal salvation. Individuals were to act morally not because of the intrinsic worth of moral action, but because by acting morally they would finally be rewarded. Leslie Dewart has named this phenomenon "spiritual hedonism".[24] Christianity consequently became subject to the charge of hypocrisy—it did not really show to humankind a morally or spiritually superior way of life, it merely exhorted the individual to forsake pleasure in this life in return for greater pleasure in the next one. Retributive theory, with its emphasis on punishment and reward, both leads to and stems from such a punishment/reward understanding of Christianity.

Such a conception of Christianity, however, is totally inadequate for any viable Christian approach to the problem of criminal justice in two ways. First, on a pastoral level, as indicated before, prisoners are highly critical of the hypocrisy of organized religion. Many prisoners are quick to point out that "acting moral" for the sake of avoiding eternal damnation is no more noble than obeying the law simply because one is afraid of going to prison. Many an inmate has been heard to claim that most "straights" would act in a criminal way except that they are afraid of punishment. In this vein, criminals often perceive themselves as having more personal integrity than non-criminals, because at least they were honest enough to act on the basis of what they felt and to accept the consequences. At the same time, some prisoners who have been exposed to fundamentalism, and many who exhibit a high degree of political consciousness, interpret such "pie-in-the-sky" Christianity as not simply foolish, but also as a means of social control which keeps the lower classes in their place by promising them a reward in the next life. Unfortunately, as is the case with many social observations by prisoners, this criticism of Christianity is frequently all too accurate. For, as long as Christianity continues to be understood and preached in this way, it will fail to be true to the spirit of the New Testament, and to heed its real calling. At the same time, as long as Christianity is understood in such terms, it will be of little interest to the majority of prisoners.

Second, a Christianity riddled with spiritual hedonism has disturbing social implications. A major contemporary problem, deeply entangled with that of criminal justice, is the tendency toward excessive individualism, whereby people make decisions on the basis of what will bring them the most personal gain. The idea of desert flourishes in a society where individuals are considered separate entities in competition with one another.[25] Thus, ultimately retribution theory encourages a destructive individualism. If Christian theology embraces a retributive model, with its primary emphasis on personal reward, then instead of acting as a catalyst encouraging the growth of community, it will serve to reinforce existing social attitudes. If Christian theology is to have any impact on American culture, one would certainly hope that it would lead people toward increased interrelationships and concern for one another, and away from personal isolationism.

Objections to Deterrence

The most frequently employed contemporary justification for punishment of criminals is the concept of deterrence. As Chicago's Norval Morris writes:

> Every criminal law system in the world, except one, (Greenland) has deterrence as its primary and essential postulate. It figures most prominently throughout our punishing and sentencing decisions, legislative, judicial and administrative.[26]

Briefly described, the theory of deterrence maintains that the punishment of criminals is justified because it deters (i.e. inhibits or restrains) both the criminal who is punished, and those who witness his/her punishment, from committing crimes in the future.

In deterrence theory, both crime and punishment are viewed as being evil. However, to the extent that punishment can be employed to deter future crime, either by the criminal himself/herself, or by others who might emulate him/her, then that punishment is justified, because while it is an evil inflicted upon the offender, it is an evil which functions to prevent future evil, i.e. further commission of crime. Deterrence theorists maintain that if sufficient penalties are ascribed to particular criminal acts, then crime will be avoided by most human beings because it would not be in their rational self-interest to risk the penalties which would follow upon their breaking the law.

As deterrence theory has grown more "sophisticated", the idea of crime prevention has been refined. Deterrence is considered on two levels: general deterrence, referring to the prevention of crime by the public at large; and specific deterrence, referring to the prevention of future crime by the individual offender who is being punished.

According to the theory of general deterrence, the punishment of offenders serves as an example to others who would be inclined to commit the same or similar offenses. The potential offender, realizing the consequences of crime in view of the punishment being meted out to the already-convicted criminal, will be frightened and thereby deterred from committing crime. This concept, of punishment by example, actually operated even before formal deterrence theory came into being. Historically, such spectacles as public confinement in the stocks, floggings, and hangings were all envisioned as "inciting terror in the minds of onlookers", and thus warning them away from crime. Likewise, the widespread practice of displaying executed criminals' bodies on gibbets in public places was intended to be a deterrent to the public at large.

Specific deterrence, on the other hand, has as its purpose the prevention of the individual criminal from further crime. If an offender suffers a severe enough punishment, it is assumed that he/she will not commit crime in the future because he/she either fears punishment or because the punishment is simply not worth the benefit to be gained from committing a crime. Significantly, specific deterrence is not the same thing as "reformation", for deterrence posits no requirement that any personality change or transformation of character occur in the prisoner. Deterrence is only concerned with how effectively punishment functions to frighten or discourage criminals from future offenses, regardless of their personal history or problems.

It was on such grounds that the later penitentiary system, which had forsaken the goal of reforming criminals, justified the harsh conditions of their institutions as well as severe disciplinary measures which they employed. The obsession which many of these penologists later had with eliminating any hope of pardon for prisoners was a result of their wish to make punishment as dreadful as possible on the assumption that greater severity yields a greater deterrent effect.

This preoccupation with severity is still operative in penology today. As Franklin Zimring and Gordon Hawkins put it:

> . . . people more often seem to think in a straight line about the deterrent effect of sanctions: If penalties have a deterrent effect in one situation, they will have a deterrent effect in all; if some people are deterred by threats, then all will be deterred; if doubling a penalty produces an extra measure of deterrence then trebling the penalty will do even better . . . When confronted with a crime problem, legislators often agree that the best hope of control lies in "getting tough" with criminals by increasing penalties . . .[27]

Or, as Paul Keve wrote:

The instinctive public reaction is to wonder what

deterrent effect will be left. The natural, human and urgent feeling is that there still must be a big stink somewhere, a period of lockup in unpleasant conditions, or else crime will be uncontrolled.[28]

There is little evidence that either general or specific deterrence works.[29] Increasingly severe penalties do not reduce the general crime rate, nor do decreased penalties lead to an upswing in crime. Nor do individual offenders avoid repeating crime after having once been punished. Yet faith in deterrence remains strong.

Despite its significance, criticism of deterrence theory has not come from religious thinkers, but from philosophers (notably Immanuel Kant)[30] and penal theorists. Yet, if there is any point where Christian belief directly clashes with penal ideology, it is on this issue.

Focusing first on specific deterrence, it is unacceptable to the Christian on the grounds that it is dehumanizing. To establish this argument it is necessary: 1) to explain how and why deterrence is dehumanizing, and 2) to demonstrate that dehumanization is specifically objectionable to Christians.

Deterrence is ultimately based on a pleasure/pain model of human behavior. While this model has supposedly been refined over time, whatever verbal maneuvering one resorts to, specific deterrence finally relies on a belief that human beings primarily act to avoid pain and to seek pleasure. Based on that assumption, it calls for the infliction of pain (punishment) as the most effective (if not the only) way in which to channel human behavior along socially acceptable paths. Stripped of its rhetoric then, deterrence theory holds that human beings respond best to coercive means.

Thus, the very model of human behavior upon which deterrence theory is based is dehumanizing, in the sense that it strips human beings of the very characteristics which define them as human—namely, intellect and spirit. According to deterrence theory, human intellect is primarily the capacity of individuals to make self-serving and self-preserving choices. Human beings are accorded the same capacities as laboratory test animals—they respond to pleasure, they avoid pain.

This is a fundamentally non-Christian anthropology. For in Christian thought, human beings are not simply physical entities, they are persons. "Whenever we say that man is a person, we mean that he is more than a mere parcel of matter, more than an individual element in nature, such as is an atom, a blade of grass, a fly or an elephant."[31] As a person, "Man is an individual who holds himself in hand by his intelligence and his will."[32] In most of the Christian tradition, human beings are accorded with some ability (however limited) to recognize what is good. Given such a capability, the human person need not be approached on a strictly physical level, with coercive and brutal means, for he/she can respond on a higher level. At the same time, the human person is spiritual, bearing "the imprint of the Father of Being" and possessing "absolute dignity" by virtue of "direct relationship with the absolute".[33] In deterrence theory, such postulates are irrelevant if not absurd. Consequently, deterrence theory leads to the establishment of a penal system where human considerations—concern for the fragile sensitivities of the human person, and possibilities for growth and self-transcendence—are systematically ignored. Having assumed that people are not fully human to begin with, *the penal system then proceeds to validate that assumption* by employing methods which at times seem almost purposefully designed to strip convicts of the last vestiges of their humanity.

The logic of deterrence calls for harsh and punitive methods. The experience of imprisonment is to be made as unpleasant as possible, so that convicts will be dissuaded from committing crime in the future. Corporal punishment within prison and various tortures were employed throughout most of the nineteenth and twentieth century to enhance the punitive elements of prison life. Such practices were brutalizing enough in their own way, and continue in some prisons to this day. But suffering in prison today is far more psychological than physical, however, and the prospects for dehumanization are much greater.

It is important to give some specific meaning to the often used, but seldom understood, concept of dehumanization. In the modern prison, dehumanization takes many forms. It occurs from the loss of individuality, a loss of the sense of self-hood, which is the result of the endless regimentation of prison life. Dehumanization takes the form of a loss of self-confidence, the result of the artificial dependency on capricious authority which the prison creates. Dehumanization results from the treatment of prisoners as sub-rational human beings, whereby they are subjected to petty and apparently senseless regulation of the smallest details of their personal life, a subjection which they cannot challenge. Dehumanization results from the severance of normal human relationships between the prisoner and those people who care about him/her the most, destroying the "rootedness in healthy relationships" which "makes the world man's home".[34] Dehumanization takes the form of loss of willingness to trust other human beings and loss of the capacity to enter into loving, sharing relationships, the result of being exposed to an unnatural social setting for too long a period of time. In short, dehumanization consists of the denial of most of the human privileges and experiences which are taken for granted as comprising the essence of any human life.

It is not enough, however, to simply recognize the psychological destruction and dehumanization which is wrought in prisons. It is necessary to move a step further and recognize that prisons involve spiritual dehumanization as well. If Vistor Frankl communicated anything from his experiences in concentration camps during World War II, it was that incarceration assaults the human spirit.[35] Continual subjection to dreadful physical conditions, to endless routine, to unfilled time, senseless coercion, to unspeakable brutality, all combine to kill the human spirit—to convince individuals that there is no hope for the future, that human life has no meaning or worth. It is this subjection of the human spirit which is the ultimate tragedy of prisons. The subjection of the human spirit, the destruction of prisoners' will to strive and resist, is an unequivocal goal of American prisons. Nineteenth century warden Elam Lynd's dictate that to reform criminals "you must first break their spirit" is still a motivating principle of American penology. As much as anything, prisons are designed to destroy convicts' will to resist. ". . . the only way to really make it with the bosses is to withdraw into yourself, both mentally and physically—literally making yourself as small as possible . . . They want you to make no waves in prison and they want you to make no waves when you get out".[36] The effectiveness of this strategy is reflected in the fatalism, the listlessness and the purposelessness one sees in the lives of so many prisoners.

Thus, the penal system, assuming that criminals are not human, then proceeds to dehumanize them. The objection to so-called deterrent punishment is not just that it fails to deter crime and "reform" prisoners, but that it is of such a character as to virtually assure that prisoners will not grow, and in effect regress in terms of human growth. If we say that prisons are "colleges of crime" it is not because prisoners learn better criminal techniques while there. It is because prisons are so humanly destructive that crime is what they must inevitably produce. Thus, deterrence theory is a self-perpetuating, destructive circle. In assuming people to be less than human, it works to make them so. What's more, for as long as people accept the "anthropology" on which deterrence is based, that human beings respond only to rewards and threats, then it will continue to appear logical to subject criminals to increasingly harsh and dehumanizing punishments, all in the name of deterrence. And as has been the case in the past, whenever steps are taken which would allow for humanity to surface within our penal system, such efforts will be rejected as not having "sufficient deterrent value".

Why is dehumanization of the human person in opposition to Christian belief? In this context, Christianity is understood as a creed which is vitally concerned with the fullest possible human development of the individual person; a creed which requires that one become fully human, not super-human. It has often been interpreted as a religion which denigrates the human person, one which is preoccupied with the suppression of sinful humankind. Yet this is a misconception, for the central fact of Christian history is that God so loved humankind that he became human himself. As Karl Barth expressed it: "Man is the measure of all things, since Jesus Christ became man."[37] The prevention of human growth, and the dehumanization of the human person, are fundamentally opposed to the Christian faith. As Irenaeus of Lyon proclaimed: "God's glory is man fully alive". For it is in human history, and in the human person, that the process of salvation takes place. Properly understood, humanization is a thoroughly Christian task, and conversely, opposition to ideologies and social systems which prevent persons from realizing their humanity becomes a Christian duty. Hence, deterrence theory, and the dehumanization which it inevitably fosters, is incompatible with Christian belief.

Turning to general deterrence, it is important to recognize that it is based on a utilitarian model of morality. Such a model maintains that it as morally acceptable for the individual human person to be used against his/her will, and without regard for him/her as a unique person, in the attainment of some larger social goal. Thus, the individual criminal may be legitimately exploited by society (an exploitation which takes the form of harsh and excessive sentences) on the grounds that it may serve to prevent future crime by members of the public at large. The argument advanced here against general deterrence is that whatever Christianity proclaims (despite its many distortions), it certainly does not approach human existence from a utilitarian point of view. On the contrary, Christianity approaches human life rooted in an acceptance of the unique value and sanctity of the individual human life.

In addition to approaching human beings in terms

of their "personhood", Christianity as a historical force exerted great pressure toward the recognition of inherent human dignity, human worth and human rights. This influence was reflected in the political and social development of western culture. Christian belief first affected classical culture.

> . . . the *humane* interest in the individual undoubtedly dates back to lines of thought in the conception of life of classical antiquity, although classical antiquity hardly attained a humanitarian culture. Both Greeks and Romans maintained an attitude to work and to woman and child that does not reveal any great esteem for human rights and human dignity: and the line between freeborn men and slaves was sharply drawn and unbridgeable.
> The new conception of the individual arrived with Christianity. When Christian principles gained influence in the dissolving Roman Empire, a new world began to rise out of the debris.[38]

In this study, much of the review of Christian influence on western culture has been critical of it. As a balance, in this context it is important to recognize that, whatever the excesses of the Middle Ages, modern historical research shows that it was a time of positive achievement. "Slavery, at least in its worst forms, was abolished; physical labor gained acceptance; woman was granted an individual value and such acts as putting out newborn children to die were made criminal offenses. Laws of justice and of peace were to regulate the relations between individuals in social life. Human dignity was being given increasing value and to the great builders of society the goal was to create peace and justice . . ."[39] In short, human beings were conceived of as ends in themselves, not simply means in a larger social plan.

In Roman Catholic theology, the worth of the human person was rooted in natural law theory, which held that the human person possessed a dignity anterior to society, and had certain rights which were his/her birthright as a human being, independent of prevailing social structures. Protestant theology, while suspicious of the natural law tradition, and more pessimistic about human nature because of its emphasis on the radical nature of sin, nonetheless developed a tradition of human rights based upon each individual's having been created by God.

Thus, Christianity has a tradition which strongly maintains the ultimate worth of each individual, a worth which cannot be lightly overlooked for the achievement of some social end. General deterrence theory, on the other hand, finds it acceptable to use individual members of society for the sake of the whole, and to achieve the goal of social order. As Hardy Goransson, former Director General of the Swedish National Prison Board wrote:

> From the crass viewpoint of social utility, many people are "worthless"—in fact, this word is much too vague, the truth being that many individuals are physically, mentally or morally a burden to society and sometimes a permanent and heavy one. There exists no rational reason to provide for them or to provide expensive care . . . Much money could be saved if one could get rid of them or at least reduce the costs of maintenance to the minimum.[40]

What general deterrence theory attempts is to take the "worthless" of American society—the criminals—and justify their continued existence by putting them to good use, the prevention of further crime.

This, as Immanuel Kant saw, violates the innate worth of the human person: "Punishment can never be administered merely as a means for promoting another Good, either with regard to the criminal himself or to Civil Society . . . For one man ought never to be dealt with merely as a means subservient to the purpose of another, nor be mixed up with the subjects of Real Right (i.e. goods and property)."[41] More significantly, general deterrence locates the worth of the human person within the prevailing social structures of the day, and evaluates the worth of the individual in terms of those structures, which are in themselves to be condemned. This clashes with the Christian view of the individual, for as Reinhold Niebuhr wrote: "According to the Christian faith, the human spirit in its freedom is finally bound only by the will of God, and the secret of its heart is only fully known and judged by divine wisdom. This means that human life has an ultimate religious warrant for transcending the custom of tribes, rational rules of conduct, and all general and abstract norms of behavior."[42]

Aside from the Christian tradition, there is an obvious difficulty in reconciling a utilitarian social attitude with the highly personalistic ministry of Jesus in the New Testament. One of the distinguishing marks of Jesus was his concern for the socially outcast and useless, and willingness to approach them as people, without regard to social standing or convention. Surely there was nothing in Jewish social conventions to justify associating with tax collectors and publicans, with lepers and adulterers. Part of the scandal of Jesus associating with such people was probably the fact that his actions could be interpreted as condoning their activity. Was he not setting a bad example for the community at large? Was he not implying that one could engage in sinful behavior without fear of condemnation? Was he not therefore encouraging lawlessness? What "deterrent value" could law and social custom have if a man like Jesus ignored their condemnations and associated with such people as if they weren't sinners? Obviously Jesus' concern far surpassed the social exigencies of the moment. He was focused on something far more important than custom, law and order. He was focused on the human person as created by God.

In this context, once when Jesus was gathered with "many tax collectors and outcasts", he was criticized by the Pharisees and teachers of the Law. In response to them, Jesus told the parable of the lost sheep. If a person owns a hundred sheep, and one is lost, then concern is focused on the one who is lost, so that it might be brought back to the fold. For a single sheep, the shepherd leaves the flock, although the other ninety-nine may go unattended. So too, "there will be more joy in heaven over one sinner who repents than over ninety-nine respectable people who do not need to repent." (Luke 15:1-7) The parable of the lost coin (Luke 15:8-10), the prodigal son (Luke 15:11-32), and many others make a similar point. Where general deterrence theory looks to the protection of the many, the Christian is called to see the worth of the one. Again, the purpose here is not to uncritically apply isolated segments of Scripture to modern social problems as an absolute standard of evaluation. Rather, the purpose is to shed light on the fact that the way in which the American penal system approaches reality and the way in which Christianity does, are often at odds with each other.

There is an obvious weakness in the above discussion, in that it focusses on the individual person to the exclusion of the larger question of the relationship between the individual and society, a question which is at the heart of any criminal justice system. Certainly Christianity has recognized the need for political authority and the maintenance of the social order. Likewise, it has never been so naive as to assume that all individuals can be trusted to act in a way which will further "the common good". In fact, Christianity has explicitly taught that government can legitimately use coercive power if it is for the common good. Cannot general deterrence then be justified on the grounds that it serves the common good?

The answer to this question hinges on how it is that one views the interrelationship between the individual and society, and what one means by the term "common good". In American usage, the term lends itself to two common errors in understanding. On the one hand, many Americans view the goal of society as "the individual good or the mere aggregate (total) of the individual goods of each of the persons who constitute it".[43] This view of society is closely linked with the retributive outlook, where people are considered as isolated entities in competition with one another. But, as Catholic political theorist Jacques Maritain pointed out, such an understanding of society is little more than "bourgeois materialism, according to which the entire duty of society consist in seeing that the freedom of each one be respected, thereby enabling the strong freely to oppress the weak".[44] Likewise, there are some Americans who consider the common good to be whatever strengthens the society and social order as a whole. In such a view, the individual members of the society can be sacrificed for the good of the majority or the social order itself.

According to Maritain, neither of these conceptions of common good are acceptable to the Christian. In his view, the term "common good" necessarily implies mutual dependence between the individual and the community at large. The individual has a responsibility to the community, but simultaneously, the community has a responsibility to the individual. It is therefore not possible to speak in terms of the "common good" if the community consistently fails to provide for *all* of its individual members. The common good in a Christian sense is *not* the good of the majority at the expense of the individual human person. In the American system of criminal justice, we are willing to enforce the individual's responsibility to the community, and to punish him/her for failing in that responsibility, but we consistently refuse to consider the community's failure to provide for its individual members, which is often the root cause of crime. We have returned to the impasse which confronted us during our discussion of justice: it is impossible to speak meaningfully about criminal justice for as long as we refuse to include with it a discussion of social justice.

Therefore, as Maritain recognized, it is absurd to speak about the "common good" without recognizing one of its essential characteristics:

(the common good) . . . implies a *redistribution*, it must be redistributed among the persons . . . of

which the social body is made up . . . and it must
aid their development.[45]

In short, as Christians, we cannot accurately refer to
the "common good" and American criminal justice
without there first being a fundamental change in the
social inequalities which are so intimately connected
with the problem of crime.[46] To blithely accept the
concept of general deterrence as serving the common
good in any genuinely Christian sense would show a
naivete bordering on irresponsibility.

The Fallacies of Treatment Theory

In approaching treatment theory, it is necessary
to recall that psychiatry (as it is practiced *in prisons*)
tends to be highly deterministic, coercive, manipula-
tive and degrading to the prisoners. While many
pioneers in treatment of prisoners were individuals
motivated by humanitarian instincts, the rosy rhetoric
of treatment and rehabilitation should not blind us to
the fact that in reality treatment in prisons is usually no
more than "scientifically" sophisticated means employed by penal authorities to exercise control over
the lives of individual prisoners. The basic argument
advanced here against the treatment model is that, like
deterrence, in both theory and practice it dehumanizes
persons held in prison and as such is inconsistent with
a truly Christian perspective on life.

Treatment theory is dehumanizing first in that it
strips the human person of his/her creative moral
powers of freedom and responsibility. Freedom, as Dr.
Victor Frankl has observed, must mean freedom in the
face of both instincts and environment:

Certainly man has instincts, but these instincts do not have him. We have nothing against instincts, nor against a man's accepting them. But . . . such acceptance must also presuppose the possibility of rejection. In other words, there must be freedom of decision . . . As for environment, we know that it does not make man, but that everything depends on what man makes of it, on his attitude toward it.[47]

Yet on both of these points treatment theorists would vigorously disagree. Criminals are conceived of as being at the mercy of their instincts, or of environmental forces surrounding them. They are not viewed as having any possible control over their lives, and therefore, cannot be considered responsible human beings. In short, they are not conceived of as having the same basic human capabilities for free thought and action as are accorded to people who have not been formally designated as "criminal". Criminals are different; they are less than fully human.

The significance of the powers of freedom and responsibility for human beings cannot be overestimated. They are creative powers in that they enable individuals to define themselves, to discover themselves in the decisions which they make for their lives. By choosing one course of action over another, and by being accountable for that choice, the individual makes a statement about his/her identity, about who he/she is trying to be as a person. To deny individuals such powers is to deny them the possibility of human growth.

Freedom and responsibility are also moral powers, in that they allow for meaning in life. Unless individuals can freely make decisions, then all human life is determined and has no spiritual meaning. Human beings would not be people, beings with "personality", but mere physical entities. This denial of personhood is particularly important in contemporary American prisons, where convicts often find meaning for their lives in resistance to the oppression which they are suffering. Treatment theory denies that prisoners can make meaningful (moral) decisions and thus is a convenient explanation for the resistance of militant prisoners, as well as a justification for subjecting them to disciplinary measures such as solitary confinement, ostensibly for "therapeutic" purposes. The logic of treatment theory dictates that prisoners who do not conform, who are hostile or create disturbances, are merely displaying symptoms of their mental illness. (A prisoner who "acts out" naturally must be "sick".) By denying that prisoners have the moral power inherent in human freedom and responsibility, treatment theory effectively undercuts resistance to the oppressive and dehumanizing realities of imprisonment. Certainly there are some few individuals in prisons who, at a given point in time, do not appear capable of free and responsible actions. But the widespread application of such a model to all criminals degrades and dehumanizes.

Having assumed that prisoners are less than fully human, and incapable of self-definition, what treatment and rehabilitation then intend to do are remake the personality of the prisoner, to substitute a new "reformed" character for his/her diseased one, and to structure for the prisoner an entirely new way of life. As one social scientist wrote in *Medical Opinion and Review*: ". . . the inmate or probationer may not only need restructuring of his heart and mind but of his life".[48] The extreme methods this type of thinking can lead to were reviewed before.

In the final analysis then, what treatment theory is really concerned with is manipulation. It attempts to shape and control the human personality along "socially acceptable lines", without regard to the individual prisoner's freedom or integrity as a person. But such manipulation, as theologian Bernard Haring points out, is objectionable to the Christian:

> The final concern and criterion in discussing manipulation is human freedom . . . (Man) has to gain the inner freedom to be, to love, to adore. He must not allow anyone to manipulate him in his inner sanctuary, his conscience, his self-interpretation, and his reaching out for meaning and for significant personal relationships.[49]

To manipulate people is to deny their God-given dignity, to treat them as "things". To manipulate them is to deny that they have standing before God as "co-creators", as beings who are capable of what is specifically human-creative, free and responsible action. Manipulation of the human person therefore is inconsistent with Christian belief. For, as Haring points out, "the Christian ideals of development in freedom, awareness and love" are anti-manipulative.[50]

Finally, treatment theory is dehumanizing in that it fosters false and ultimately crippling conceptions of the human person. In reality, individuals are not wholly determined beings, and they are capable of a fully human life. This applies equally to human beings on both sides of the prison walls. To fail to recognize this is to do irreparable damage to the people who are trapped within our prisons. An insight from Victor Frankl pertains to this point:

> If we present a man with a concept of man which is not true, we may well corrupt him. When we present man as an automaton of reflexes, as a mind-machine, as a bundle of instincts, heredity, and environment, we feed the nihilism to which modern man is, in any case, prone.[51]

When we tell prisoners that they are sick individuals, who are not capable of free and responsible human existence, we corrupt them. We also feed the despair and self-hatred and emptiness to which they are, based on their experiences, already prone. The problem is not simply that it is inaccurate to classify criminals in terms of treatment theory. Rather the problem is that it is positively harmful to them as human beings. Again it is important to emphasize that dehumanization is not simply a fancy term—it is a terrible reality as well. Perhaps the most destructive product of the American penal system is the prisoners' acceptance of the various dehumanizing labels which are pinned on them to "explain away" not simply their criminality, but their identity as human beings as well. Much criminal behavior is the direct result of the dehumanization which accompanies the experience of being processed through the American penal system. For, once human beings come to view themselves as inhuman or deranged individuals, then that self-understanding affects every aspect of their lives. And the prisoner who sees himself/herself as inhuman, will usually try to confirm that belief by doing inhuman things.[52] (In this context it is interesting to note how treatment personnel in prisons are so obsessed with having prisoners accept the diagnosis of themselves as sick. One of the rationales for the indeterminate sentence is that it keeps the criminal in custody until he/she is willing to submit to treatment.) Thus, as was the case with deterrence, treatment theory begins with the presupposition that prisoners are less than human, and then proceeds to validate that assumption by vigorous striving to influence prisoners to accept such beliefs about themselves.

In addition to the relatively obvious objection that treatment theory and practice are ultimately dehumanizing, there is a more subtle argument for rejecting the treatment approach to the problem of crime. In a certain sense, it can be said that the treatment approach is an attempt by sinful, fallible human beings to assume God-like powers of judgment over fellow human beings, and at the same time to implicitly endorse an American materialist, technological culture as being in some way "ultimate". Interpreted in this way, the treatment model might well be construed as a modern manifestation of idolatry, and a frightening parallel to the mythical "sin" in the book of Genesis.

Hard-line proponents of the treatment ethic do not merely expect the courts to make simple decisions as to the guilt or innocence of criminals in a narrow, legal sense. Nor do they expect penal authorities to simply punish or teach prisoners. Rather, they see the courts as a preventive mechanism for isolating unfit individuals, and the prisons as places where the personalities of such undesirables are to be altered.[53] Such decisions are much more momentous and dangerous than earlier legal verdicts as to an individual's guilt or innocence. They endow legal and penal officials with awe-some power over the very personal identity of individual human beings. As our technical expertise at altering personalities and shaping the human mind grows, so too does our power to alter the existence of human beings in previously inviolate, even sacred areas. In prisons where frontal lobotomies, sensory deprivation, drug therapy and other scientifically dehumanizing technologies are employed, prisoners are being more than punished. Their integrity and identity as human beings is being tampered with. As governmental programs designed to alter personality structures are funded and tested in American prisons, correctional personnel and "therapists" are confronted with previously undreamed of capacities for evil. By what right do we give human beings such power?

In the Genesis myth, man and woman were given access to all things which were God's, except one—complete knowledge, including absolute knowledge of good and evil. Because of this limitation, humankind was dependent upon God. In eating from the tree of knowledge, man and woman rejected their dependent status and attempted to possess absolute knowledge, which was denied to them. Viewed broadly, their sin was the refusal to acknowledge their contingent nature, their inability to hold and exercise divine knowledge and power. Extreme defenders of modern treatment theory, enchanted by the possibilities of personality and behavior modification, urge us to repeat this sin. As God created man and woman in his image and likeness, behavioral theorists would return the favor by re-creating criminals in prison to *their* image and likeness.[54] The arrogance of these efforts is surpassed only by the naive belief that such absolute power in the hands of human beings will not inevitably lead to corruption.

The psychiatric approach to life in general, as Thomas Szasz has observed, is a kind of religion, the creed of which is prevailing American, middle-class values of security, conformity, docility, etc., which American psychiatry tends to endorse.[55] In prisons, the task of the treatment staff, or therapist, is to convert or coerce the criminal into accepting this "religion". The ultimate norm in such a system is whether or not the individual prisoner adapts to the demands of the prevailing social structure. The real goal of treatment becomes remaking the lower, criminal class into the middle-class. If he/she does not adapt, then more persuasive/coercive means are employed. In the long run, the logic of such an approach dictates that more and more powerful means ought to be employed, until we move "beyond freedom and dignity" and ensure social conformity and efficiency regardless of the human cost.

In the final analysis, therefore, the treatment "gospel" advocates an American, middle-class system of values and life-style as the standard for all human beings. Inasmuch as this is true, social structures and prevailing social mores are endowed with an ultimacy which they do not deserve. In a very real sense this is a form of idolatry, understood as being a process whereby something temporal and human is given an absolute character which, by its very nature, it is not entitled to. This tendency, to consider contemporary knowledge and social institutions as final and ultimately valid, is evident throughout the history of human attempts to confront the problem of criminal justice. Certainly the medieval Church felt secure in believing that it possessed the best "answer" to the problem of crime: as well as the Reformers, the Quakers, the Puritans, the early Americans, defenders of the penitentiary, etc. The failure to maintain a truly human humility in the face of the problem of evil has led to countless cruelties in the name of truth. The modern treatment movement, with its glorification of profane technological American society, repeats this error. Only, the idol is draped with the mantle of "science", as opposed to the earlier tendency to disguise human idols with more traditional religious symbols.

Christian attitudes toward treatment theory have great practical significance in terms of the Christian pastoral ministry to prisoners. With the movement to professionalize the ministry in prisons, many Christian clergy were moved to embrace treatment theory as a means of improving their effectiveness as ministers. However, many of them did so without clearly examining what kinds of treatment theory are compatible with Christian belief, and what kinds are inconsistent. In some institutions, where chaplains were re-organized as part of the "treatment team", their effectiveness as ministers of God, as opposed to representatives of American society, was jeopardized.

An example serves to illustrate the problem. In the late 1960's and early 1970's a number of prison chaplains began experimenting with a counseling method known as "reality therapy".[56] The great strength of this method was that it insisted each individual exercise what freedom he/she had in life and take responsibility for his/her future, thereby avoiding the major pitfall of most treatment theory, the denial of human freedom and responsibility. Reality therapy also implies, however, that the prevailing social structure is just and good, and if a person is in trouble with the law it is because they did something wrong and acted irresponsibly. The goal of reality therapy is therefore to have prisoners adapt to society at large. The problem with such an approach is that it abandons the Christian's role as social critic, as a prophetic witness against social injustice, and conceives of the Christian ministry in the very limited sense of having sinners "repent" (i.e. give-in to the demands of American society). What we are then left with is the basic failing of Christian thinking on criminal justice, the tendency to approach criminal and social justice as separate issues.

Certainly there is much to be learned from the social sciences and from psychiatry. A fundamentalist perspective on Christianity, which rejects all insights from these disciplines as misguided or sinful is something to avoid. But many Christians have been mistaken in naively assuming that the comforting rhetoric of treatment theory is easily reconciled with the truly radical mission of the church of Jesus Christ.

5
THE FAILURE OF
CHRISTIAN WITNESS

If in fact much of penal ideology is inconsistent with Christian belief, then the disquieting question arises as to why Christianity has been such a source of support for the American criminal justice and penal systems, and why there has not been great interest among Christians in transforming them. This chapter considers Christian support of these systems as a failure of Christian witness, both in the church,[1] and in Christian theology. In this regard, it is important to recall that one of the functions of theology is critical reflection on the life of the Church, as it is called and addressed by the Word of God. The Church itself is "a pilgrim", progressing toward the Kingdom, without fully possessing it.[2] As such, the Church must continually undergo self-criticism, in order to renew itself, and dedicate itself anew to its task of serving the Kingdom of God, lest it lose touch with its roots and serve exclusively the kingdom of men.

The following criticism of Christianity is in no way meant to imply that the church and theology have completely failed in their witness; that they have been totally submissive to the demands of culture and government; that they have never spoken for the oppressed; or, that individual Christians have not been at times heroically faithful to their beliefs. Such a position is obviously false. On the other hand, viewed in broad historical perspective it is undeniable that Christianity has been a source of support for much of the demonic in American history, particularly with respect to criminal justice, and has provided much force and legitimacy for institutions which have ultimately been proven destructive of the human person and the human community. For the Church and Christian theologians to confront the failure of American criminal justice, they must first honestly confront their own role in contributing to that failure.

Failures to Bear Witness in the Church

Since the time of Constantine, Christianity has been deeply immersed in Western political and social culture.[3] The largely negative consequences of this alliance, for the Church's credibility and for its mission with respect to criminal justice, were illustrated in chapter two. Christianity became a legitimizing force for many social injustices and repressive means of social control, and frequently lost sight of its essential message of reconciliation for all people. In the American experience, despite the much-proclaimed formal, legal separation of Church and state, the cultural alliance between Christianity and government has continued, particularly concerning criminal justice, and the consequences for the Church have once again been largely negative.

To many, the American way of life, with all of its materialist and technological perversions, and its middle-class ethic of individualism and social stability, is completely consistent with Christian belief. Political institutions and social structures are seen as divinely sanctioned. Such an understanding of Christianity would have us believe that to be a good Christian means to be a good American—a law-abiding, tax-paying, God-fearing, middle-class citizen. Christianity and American "civil religion" become virtual equals.

A major problem with this popular, Americanized approach to Christianity is that it provides no place for people who do not fit well within the prevailing social order, or for people who are a threat to it, such as criminals. It fails to speak to the experience of large segments of the American people because:

> The fact is that the very poor and minorities whose bounds are defined by the affluent and accepted classes have not been socialized to that natural sense of belongingness. Their God, if they have a God, is not the God of civil religion . . . The "effervescence" of civil religion is not a social universal across all class lines, nor across all ethnic lines . . . (the poor and minorities) have never really belonged. And they have never really belonged because they have never had a share of the society's resources.[4]

The tragedy of the identification of Christianity with the interests of the "established" in American society is that, whenever it has happened, it has led the church to betray its mission and to lose touch with its roots. For, Christianity was originally preached by its founder and his disciples as a religion for the social outcasts, for the weak, the poor, the hated, the forgotten—the prisoner. The unique power of Christianity was its concern for the unwanted as individual human beings, and its unconcern with social status and the preservation of the status quo.

Therefore, in the words of Marie Augusta Neal, of Harvard Divinity School, Christianity "could never be genuinely a civil religion unless the nation were a nation of all human beings relating to each other as peers. Using Christian symbols for any particular national solidarity is a co-optation of a religious experience, a religious tradition and religious ministry".[5] Whenever Christianity and Christian symbols have been used to legitimize any particular social or political structures or institution, the Christian church has failed to be true to its calling. And in the American experience such co-optations have been nowhere more prevalent than in the field of criminal justice.

Throughout its history, the Christian Church in America has endorsed, tacitly approved, or at the very least been shamefully ignorant of the inhumanities of our criminal justice system. Even after the explicitly religious penal models of the penitentiary movement have faded into history, it was (and is) widely assumed that the punishment of criminals is in some way a holy duty. Christians have, as a rule, plainly declared themselves as strongly in favor of "law and order", despite the fact that, as J. Edgar Hoover himself once candidly admitted, "Justice is incidental to law and order". And where Christians have been concerned with justice, it has all too frequently been the selective vengeance we have sanctioned as retribution, as opposed to the all-encompassing righteousness which is known as justice in the bible. It is not at all unusual to hear a Christian minister decry the rising tide of crime and immorality in print or in the pulpit, but it is rare indeed to hear a Christian minister exhorting the faithful to actually dare to love their enemies. On the subject of criminal justice, most American Christians embrace what H.

Richard Niebuhr has described as the "Christ of culture". Hence, they "feel no great tension between Church and world, the social laws and the Gospel, the working of divine grace and human effort, the ethics of salvation and the ethics of social conservation and progress . . . they harmonize Christ and culture, not without excision, of course, from New Testament and social customs, of stubbornly discordant features".[6] In short, the plainly destructive, dehumanizing and thoroughly un-Christian institutions of criminal justice have been supported, endorsed and even sanctified by the various Christian denominations and individual Christians as well.

The attitude of many Christians (Catholic and Protestant alike) toward the problems of law and criminal justice are aptly summarized in the words of Catholic Cardinal John Wright:

> . . . as order is Heaven's first law, so law is the condition, the essential condition, of order on earth.
> So intimately bound up with one another are the laws of the land and the laws of God, that he who mocks the one undermines the other, while he who serves either becomes the noble servant of both.[7]

The law, and by extension the institutions of the criminal justice system which are entrusted with the task of maintaining order on earth, are endowed with a sacral character which obscures the various inhumanities which are perpetrated by them. It is simply assumed that the criminal law, and the social order which it defends are just and righteous; are something which the Christian can be comfortable with. Likewise, it is implied that those who violate that order, the criminals, transgress not simply against human laws but against God or "Justice" as well. Thus the extraordinary suffering with which criminals and the oppressed in general are afflicted becomes more palatable. It appears to be legitimate; even deserved. One can be a Christian and still not lose sleep over the inequalities and brutalities which still afflict American society. Rather than serve as a challenge to the inadequacies of American social and criminal justice, a force for the transformation of the institutions of American society, Christianity becomes an extension of the very kind of society it was founded in opposition to.

The cause of this merger of Christian and American ideals is not at all clear. To a larger extent than it might at first seem, popular thinking on criminal justice stems back to the medieval age of Christendom, when Church and state were virtually identical.

Likewise, we persist in the Puritan assumption that in the administration of criminal law and punishment the forces of right prevail and the forces of evil, represented by criminals, are repressed. Regardless of its causes, however, the close relationship between the Christian religion and prevailing social structures has had some injurious consequences for both the Church and American society. As historian Christopher Dawson has observed about the connection between religion and culture:

> . . . If this identification is carried to its extreme conclusion, the marriage of religion and culture is equally fatal to either partner, since religion is so tied to the social order it loses its spiritual charac-

ter, and the free development of culture is restricted by the bonds of religious tradition until
the social organism becomes as rigid and lifeless
as a mummy.[8]

Certainly the development of a more humane and truly
Christian response to the problem of crime in America
has been restricted by our civil religion, cultural myths,
and the many interpretations of "Christianity" which
have nourished them. Our system of criminal justice is
shrouded with so much myth that it is the proverbial
"sacred cow" which no one dares to destroy. In spite
of its all too apparent failure, it seems to exist independently of efforts to tame or re-direct it. More significant, however, is the effect which the alliance of
Christianity and American culture has had on the
Church. As Marie Neal points out, whenever Christianity serves primarily those with relative social
power and wealth, it not only betrays its mission to
stand with the outcast, but actually loses touch with
the transcendent itself, because "the God that these
people (then) worship is the very society that serves
their advantage in laws that protect property rights
rather than human rights".[9]

This failure of the church is basically a failure to
be true to its prophetic mission. The Christian church
has not served as a sign of God's judgment upon the
human and transitory, as a sign of a new order in
which all that seems so important in the eyes of humans (e.g. social standing, material wealth, et. al.) is
really unimportant in the eyes of God. Rather, the
Church has too often aligned itself with the old order,
so as to prop it up. Far from ushering in a new age,

wherever the church has failed in its prophetic mission, it has actually prolonged the old. It is this failing of the church which has lost it so much credibility among those (including prisoners) who do not share in the fruits of the current age, and therefore hunger for the coming of a "new being".

The weakness of the church's prophetic witness on the subject of criminal justice is apparent even in its recent attempts to confront the issue. For instance, the Lutheran Church of America's 1972 statement "In Pursuit of Justice and Dignity" states its prime concern as being the "growing incidence of lawlessness" and "unchecked criminal behavior".[10] It wishes to see the criminal justice system reformed primarily so that there will be an upswing in "public confidence that security is being maintained". There is little sense of outrage or indignation about the basic inhumanity of the penal system. Or, for instance, the 1973 statement of the U.S. Catholic Conference hedges when faced with the possibility of direct criticism of the criminal justice system, merely saying: "We need to examine whether we *may not have* a 'poor man's' system of criminal justice."[11] These examples could be multiplied. The point is that the church has been so timid in its criticism that it has still failed to confront the real issues. "I was in prison . . ." and you convened a prestigious task-force of leading citizens and authorities, which, after much "vigorous and penetrating discussion" issued a truly "responsible" statement on criminal justice which recognized the "complexity" of the issues involved and made "balanced" suggestions for "reform", whereupon it adjourned amidst self-congratulation at the "progress" which had been made. Moreover, as the prophetic literature grows, we would do well to remember that talk is cheap, and as William Stringfellow warns:

> There is simply a point at which social analysis must be validated in action or else it becomes morbid, self-indulgent and misleading, compounding the very issues it professes to clarify. There comes a moment when words must either become incarnated or the words, even if literally true, are rendered false.[12]

Failure to Bear Witness in Theology

Just as the Christian Church has failed to adequately come to grips with the problem of criminal justice, so too Christian theologians and thinkers have often neglected or exacerbated the problem. Theology is an important source of either criticism or support for prevailing religious and cultural myths and social structures. In terms of criminal justice, the problem with Christian theology stems both from what it has done, and what it has not done.

> In the fierce power play of society the theologian has usually ended up on top with the high and mighty, legitimating the status quo. For centuries in the United States only a few have taken a hard look at the difference between the originative events of the Christian faith in Jesus of Nazareth and the secular power play in which theology is caught . . . Even if theology did not always fall prey to power, it seldom was critical of it. We have had (biblical) form criticism, and redaction

criticism, criticism of almost every kind, but little *ideology criticism.*[13]

With respect to criminal justice, Christian theology has fostered an uncritical attitude on the part of Christians toward political power and the state. As Reinhold Niebuhr pointed out, both Catholic and Protestant theology have with few exceptions consistently misinterpreted Paul's letter to the Romans as a wholesale endorsement of the divine function of political authority.[14]

> Everyone must obey the state authorities, because no authority exists without God's permission, and the existing authorities have been put there by God. Whoever opposes the existing authority opposes what God has ordered; and anyone who does so will bring judgment on himself. For rulers are not to be feared by those who do good, but by those who do evil. Would you like to be unafraid of the man in authority? Then do what is good and he will praise you. For he is God's servant working for your own good. But if you do evil, be afraid of him, because his power to punish is real. He is God's servant and carries out God's wrath on those who do evil. (Romans 13:1-5)

This one isolated text from scripture has provided the basis for almost all orthodox teaching on law and punishment in the major Christian traditions. Combined with later Christian teaching on the need for political authority to save sinful humankind from self-annihilation, this passage has helped to give divine legitimacy to the institutions of government.

Yet, reliance on this tradition for the construction of a Christian stance on criminal justice is inadequate. First, scripture scholars have long since discarded the notion that Paul's letter can correctly be interpreted in such a literal way. It must be viewed in the historical context in which it was written as well as in the general context of Paul's other teaching and the New Testament as a whole.[15] More significantly, however, history has shown us that a literal interpretation of Paul's words leads to a gross error. For governments have frequently assumed demonic forms and been forces for evil as opposed to ministers of God. In America, Christians are just beginning to recognize, on any widespread scale, that the claims of the Gospel and the claims of the state may come into conflict. Certainly the Vietnam war was a moment of "kairos" for many. For others, the issue of government-sponsored abortions has been a turning point in their consciousness.

The 1971 prison riot at the Attica State Prison in New York was a turning point for many people's understanding of criminal justice.[16] At Attica, the lives of forty-three, prisoners, and guards being held as hostages, were lost when state authorities refused to accept a list of prisoners' legitimate grievances about conditions at the prison and used force to put down the uprising. The horror of the situation was compounded when, after suppressing the revolt, prison authorities ruthlessly beat and otherwise physically abused the prisoners involved. What affected people most about Attica, however, was the fact that the prisoners' involved, even in the face of their own death, did not harm their hostages; that the prison guards were killed not by the inmates but by state police bullets; and most significantly, that the authorities then lied about the true cause of the hostages' death and claimed they had been mutilated in an attempt to cast the innocent prisoners as inhuman beasts who deserved their fate. During the Attica uprising, via television and the press, many Americans encountered prisoners as human beings for the first time. Simultaneously, when the truth about the riot became known, many Americans recognized that the truly criminal actions which took place were not committed by the prisoners, but by those who were sworn to uphold the law. Attica stands as a reminder to American Christians and non-Christians alike that naive assumptions about the depravity of the people we call criminals, and about the righteousness of the state in its exercise of power, are dangerously irresponsible. After Attica, to seriously consider a literal interpretation of Romans 13 as an acceptable foundation for Christian thinking on criminal justice would be gross self-deception, an unwillingness to see the truth as it stares us in the face.

One weakness of Christian theology is that it has never adequately come to grips with the emergence of historical consciousness—"the discovery of the temporally conditioned character of all of man's products".[17] Christian theology has long been accustomed to thinking in terms of unchanging structures and absolutes. The major institutions and practices of western culture, the law, free enterprise, male-dominated households, etc., were all believed to be fundamentally Christian in nature and reflections of some absolute standard or law. With the rise of historical consciousness in the 19th century, it became apparent that institutions once thought perfect and timeless, were in fact human and changeable. This led to a tendency to reject all moral standards as being relative, to deny the existence of any absolute norms for humankind. The church rightly opposed such thinking, and steadfastly proclaimed the existence of absolute norms. However, in rightly trying to defend the existence of absolute standards for human beings to follow, the church has often wrongly defended *particular* political and social institutions such as the criminal law and has lost credibility as a result. For instance, theologians are often so concerned with establishing the existence of justice as an absolute standard—as timeless, unwavering, divine—that they completely overlook the perversion of that idea in the events of human history.

Part of the problem with Christian political theology in general, as Jacques Ellul points out in his *False Presence of the Kingdom*, is that it is often dreadfully naive.[18] Many Christian writers are predisposed to assume that since Jesus is "Lord of history", that "evil" has been vanquished for "good", and that historical, human institutions such as governments, legal systems and prisons will therefore necessarily serve the "good"; Christians need feel no great tension with the world, for the world has been reconciled to Christ. Certainly American Christian defenders of prisons have naively assumed that their well-intentioned reform measures will necessarily succeed in spite of the inherently destructive character of prisons. Likewise, Church leaders who have embraced the criminal law as the answer to the moral paradoxes of crime have rather simplistically assumed that the law itself could not be used in perverse and truly criminal ways. For as Ellul sardonically noted: "When Satan proposes to Jesus Christ to turn over to him the dominion over all the kingdoms of the world he is not lying. He continues to have authority over the political powers, and Jesus in no way disputes this."[19]

In this vein, Christian theologians are continually trying to devise theological justifications for law, to "baptize" law and declare it a fundamentally "Christian" institution.[20] Catholic theology tends to resort to theories of natural law. Protestant theology usually looks for the justification of law in the "divine ordering of creation" or in Scripture. The most remarkable characteristic of all of these writings is that they have very little of anything to do with law as it actually exists and operates. Theologians enshrine the concept of law but show little concern for historical manifestations of it.

Yet this naivete on the part of Christian theologians should not be surprising. For theology, as Gustavo Gutierrez has pointed out, is something which *follows*. "Theology does not produce pastoral activity; rather it reflects upon it."[21] The failure of Christian theology is related to the broader failure of Christians to adequately identify with the socially outcast. It is easy to find a theological foundation for governmental power and for the criminal law when one has not experienced first-hand the human destruction which they can cause. Likewise, it is easy to write about the healing, purifying function of punishment if one has not personally experienced the living hell of imprisonment. As Tom Driver of Union Theological Seminary concluded:

> . . . the anemia of latter-day theological language is much due to its undernourishment from primary experience . . . we need today not more theory, but more experience, which is the source of theory.[22]

For as long as Christian thinkers and writers approach

the world and problems of human history in a detached and (literally) disinterested way; for as long as we are content to devise idealistic justifications for political and social institutions without regard to their impact on human beings; for as long as we persist in intellectualizing the Gospel and refuse to engage human beings and speak to their experience; then, Christian theology will have little to say about the real issues raised by criminal justice.

6
THE FOUNDATIONS OF A CHRISTIAN APPROACH TO CRIMINAL JUSTICE

To this point the tone of this study has been largely negative. It has primarily focused upon what is inadequate about the ways in which Americans and Christians approach the subject of criminal justice. Such criticism is indispensable groundwork, for as Reinhold Niebuhr warned, a genuinely Christian view of any social subject necessarily must be rooted in a "Christian humility which has no illusions about our ideals and structures or about the realities of the community."[1] In this chapter the focus is shifted to positive aspects of Christian revelation and tradition which can provide insights for coming to grips with the problem of crime.

It considers the question: how is Christian faith relevant to the issues and problems raised by criminal justice?

These reflections are not presented as a solution, or as a social agenda or program for answering the problem of crime. Rather, they are concerned with how to conceive of the problem; how to approach it in the light of Christian faith. In short, what this chapter presents is a faith-perspective on criminal justice.

The Love of Enemies

As part of the Sermon on the Mount, Jesus explicitly teaches that we should love our enemies. "You have heard that it was said, 'Love your friends, hate your enemies.' But now I tell you: love your enemies, and pray for those who mistreat you, so that you will become the sons of your Father in heaven." (Matt. 5:43-34) This teaching, and teachings with a similar tone and message echo throughout the New Testament. The specific command to love one's enemies, however, has particular relevance and meaning for a discussion of criminal justice.

This teaching is appropriate, first because it leaves room for the realistic recognition that criminals and people in prison are in a very tangible way enemies of the prevailing social order, and can also be enemies to the individual Christian in the sense that Christians are the victims of crime as much as anyone else. Some people who are concerned with the lot of criminals and prisoners would like to portray all of them as harmless, misunderstood victims of oppression. While it is certainly true that they are misunderstood and often victims of oppression, it is thoroughly unrealistic to suppose that most of them are harmless. While often victims of society, they are almost never completely innocent victims. And just as they are victimized, so too they prey upon others. The simple truth is that criminals and prisoners (like all human beings) can be destructive, hostile, dangerous individuals. They are capable of (if not prone to) doing unloving, even evil things. Some of them are thoroughly unlikable people, and at times it takes no small effort to see in them any "spark of the divine". None of this is meant to deny that they are human beings, or to alter any of the observations made in chapter four about prisoners. It is merely to say that refusing to recognize the harsher human realities involved in crime leads only to delusion.

Thus much of the popular liberal mythology about criminals is foolish sentimentalism. Moreover, an unwillingness to recognize the harsh reality of crime often disguises a fear of embracing the truly radical character of Christian faith. For Jesus was not so naive as to say, "do not have enemies", as well he might have. Rather he issues a much more difficult and all-encompassing command: in full awareness of the fact that you have enemies, that there are others who would do harm to you, *love them anyway*. Jesus did not deny the existence of evil. Rather, he taught that, in spite of it, we should return evil with good. Only by recognizing this can we capture the true meaning of the Gospel message. Sentimentalism and naivete are really subtle means of "watering-down" Jesus' teaching.

Aside from being realistic, the concept of enmity is useful in approaching the problem of crime in that it is a relational concept: it refers to how it is that individuals or groups of individuals stand in relation to one another. It indicates whether they are reconciled, or whether they are at odds. Enmity, properly understood, is not a term which labels or categorizes; which attempts to make final and irrevocable statements about the way in which individuals stand in relation to one another. Rather, it implies the possibility of change in human relationships. For today's friend may be tomorrow's enemy, and vice versa.

American culture readily accepts this in international relations (shifting alliances), in inter-group relations (labor unions can now support Republicans) and in interpersonal relations (this year's marriage is next year's divorce). Yet American society steadfastly refuses to acknowledge the possibility of change with respect to the relationship between criminals and society. Once a person is judged to be a criminal in American society, he/she virtually always carries that stigma for life. One goes from being a convict to being an ex-convict, never to being a full citizen again. As ex-convicts, they cannot vote, cannot enter many professions, are discriminated against in job competition and education, etc. Americans do not see crime as a breakdown in relationships, with the possibility of there being a restoration. Rather, they use the designation "criminal" as a badge to isolate the socially undesirable, in effect to block any chance of there ever being a restored relationship between criminal and community.

To approach the problem of crime in terms of enmity, in the Christian sense, would signify opposition to the social tendency to isolate criminals and to deny them any share in the life of the community. To conceive of crime in this way would be to conceive of it as fundamentally a problem of human interrelationship. Most significantly, to consider people who commit crimes as enemies (people who are at odds with society or its members), rather than as "criminals" (inhuman beasts who are neither capable nor deserving of life with the rest of the community), is to presuppose that they and society can be reconciled; that there is a possibility for a new relationship between them—that their relationship can change from one of opposition and conflict to one of solidarity and peace.

Finally, the term "enemy" is an appropriate one to use in considering the dilemmas of crime because it is a two-edged sword. Just as "law-abiding society" may consider the criminal to be an enemy, the criminal usually considers American society and its members as his/her enemy. As the criminal is viewed by society as being destructive and a threat to its well-being, so too, society is viewed by the criminal. Failure to recognize the truth of prisoners' claim of oppression, that, in a tragically real sense society is an enemy to them, will only lead us to persist in erroneously thinking that we can reasonably demand justice from individual lawbreakers while tolerating injustice on the part of the community as a whole.

The relevance of the concept of "enemy" for conceiving of the problem of criminal justice is clearly evident and would be easily acceptable to most people. The relevance of the second element of Jesus' teaching, love, is not so easily granted. In discussing any social problem, not just crime, love is seldom if ever seriously mentioned as having any practical relevance. It is dismissed as being idealistic and sentimental, and Jesus' teaching on love is limited in its application to so-called "personal" morality.

The love-ethic is left for pious "wishing for heaven" discourses, with some passing acknowledgment that "we all wish a loving society were possible, BUT . . ." and the speaker quickly goes on to some more "realistic" discussion of power and politics . . . (Yet) the power ethic has failed to demonstrate that it serves human happiness or progress, or that it has the inevitability claimed for it. Rather we see a tragic history of misery as a result of actions based on power concepts and goals.[2]

Even apart from the fact that the "power ethic" has failed to produce very humane results, the off-hand dismissal of the relevance of love for social relations by both theologians and individual Christians is cause for unease. For what is more characteristic of both the life and the teaching of Jesus than his revelation of the all-encompassing importance of love? And what real significance can Christianity have if its "greatest two commandments" (Matt. 22:37-40), which basically proclaim the necessity of love in all things, are held to be relevant only in some areas of human life?

Bernard Haring contends that the ethic of love as expressed by Jesus in the Sermon on the Mount has a "normative" value for Christians.[3] By this he means that to the extent one takes seriously Jesus' promise of a new being in the coming Kingdom (reign) of God, then one must help to inaugurate that reign by striving to love in all things. Jesus does not so much command us to love as he does invite us to do so. The ethic of love provides direction; it points the way toward the ultimate transformation of humankind which was begun by Jesus. Viewed in this way it is not so easy to simply dismiss the relevance of love for social relations. For while rigid social structures may not allow for love, and expectation of the instant transformation of society is obviously a false hope, it is still possible to bear witness to the real possibility of love and thus point to the future realization of the promise revealed in Jesus.[4]

Yet all of this suffers from abstraction. The question remains: faced with the concrete reality of the criminal justice system, what does it mean to love one's enemies? In answer to this question, one must recognize that in order to love criminals or prisoners, it is first necessary to recognize them as human beings, who possess dignity, who deserve respect, and who have human needs and sensitivities as much as any other person. As obvious as this may appear, it is certainly not recognized in the American criminal justice system or within American society in general. On the contrary, criminals are viewed by the community and by the penal system as less than fully human and are subjected to penal practices which work to obscure all traces of their humanity. And this failure to recognize prisoners as human beings makes it impossible to think of showing love toward them. An insight of Gabriel Marcel's pertains to this point. He believes that before human beings can bring themselves to participate in, or approve of, destructive actions against others, it is first necessary for them to lose sight in their own minds of the very humanity of the people who will suffer as a consequence. "I (must) lose all awareness of the individual reality of the being whom I may be led to destroy. In order to transform him into a mere impersonal target, it is absolutely necessary to (first) convert him into an abstraction: *the* Communist, *the* anti-Facist, the Facist and so on . . ."[5] Marcel could well have added *the* criminal to his list. For the social type-casting of criminals propagated by the media, and the social scientists and the law enforcement officials, etc., works to obscure the fundamental truth that behind the various images and labels there lives a human being. The various myths about criminals make it easy *not* to love them. Considering these myths, which permeate American culture, the absence of love exhibited by the inhumanity of our penal system, and public tolerance of that inhumanity, is easy to comprehend. We show no care or concern for criminals because we do not see them as human. And recognition of a person's humanity is a precondition for the existence of love:

> If we are to love an enemy, a friend, a prisoner, a Communist, a Vietcong, or another Christian, it must be by individualizing and personalizing him . . . To come to an understanding of . . . our brothers and sisters . . . is totally different from analyzing them or imposing on them abstract ideals and principles . . . An existential knowledge of the real needs of man is very different from an abstract knowledge by which people so coldly "judge" and discriminate.[6]

Achieving such knowledge is not easy. So much of American culture works against it. Headlines and television remind us of the brutality of criminals. Textbooks tell us that they are sick. Victims stand as terrible proof of how dangerous criminals can be. And the criminals themselves are kept locked away in foreboding concrete and steel fortresses, nameless numbers with expressionless faces, whose voices seldom reach us. But, as difficult as it may be, it is nonetheless essential that we strive to see the humanity that is there.

Yet, even if we can bring ourselves to recognize that prisoners are people, what does it mean to show love toward them? A concrete beginning would be to take seriously the biblical injunction to refuse to return evil with evil, to refuse to hate criminals, and therefore to refuse to subject them to the harsh, degrading and dehumanizing conditions and practices which are part and parcel of the American penal system today. Thus, a serious attempt to show love for prisoners would necessarily involve committed opposition to the punitive ethic which fuels so much of contemporary penal practice. The urge to wreak vengeance upon criminals is the ultimate cause of brutal prison regimens and long prison sentences. Likewise, it is the force behind the movement to re-establish the death penalty. If one approached the problem of crime with an ethic of love, such means of punishment would be totally unacceptable because of the irrevocable harm which they inflict upon the human person.

Beyond opposition to brutality and destruction, an attempt to express love for criminals would also require a reaching out to them, a demonstration of care and concern for them as human beings. Such a reaching out could take many concrete forms—visits to prison, support before parole boards or in court, contact with a convict's wife and family, volunteering to teach inside of prisons, offering jobs to prisoners who are released, etc. The important element is not so much the specific action taken as the genuine concern which it signifies. One of the basic truths about many prisoners is that they fail to see any worth in themselves. They are likely to regard expressions of love as insincere, or perhaps dreadfully inappropriate because they have been conditioned to see themselves as worthless. Yet, in spite of this, a genuine expression of love can, with time, work a remarkable affect in their lives.

Still, it is naive to suggest that expressions of care

or concern will work an immediate transformation in the lives of all, or even most, prisoners. Experience in working with prisoners will rapidly prove that they, like most people, seldom find it easy to make major changes in their lives. Hence it is necessary to take notice of a third characteristic of Christian love; namely, that it is unconditional. Jesus did not teach to love others because they will then love you in return. In his own lifetime he experienced the hostility and the rejection of those toward whom he showed love. Ultimately his love for others was the cause of his death. So we are warned: the attempt to love carries no guarantee of acceptance or reward. If anything it brings grief. Hence, to make a decision to love is to make a decision to do so in spite of the price which one must pay for loving.

It is probably this last characteristic of Christian love which makes it so difficult for many Christians to comprehend the sense of loving one's enemies. For love is all too often viewed as being strictly emotion: warm feelings and good vibrations. It is not considered as something spiritual, as something more permanent than a fleeting impulse in the mind, and something more intentional than a pleasurable response to an attractive stimulus. And if love is only a feeling, it is easily drowned in the sea of conflicting emotional reactions caused by crime: fear, repulsion, hatred, fascination, temptation, compassion, etc. It is only when love is rooted in something more substantial than just emotion, when it stems from a faith commitment rooted in one's very being, that it survives in spite of traumatic incidences of crime.

To this point the ideal of "love of enemies" has been considered in terms of its relevance for the way in which Christians conceive of, and respond to, criminals. There is, however, a more subtle, but no less significant, way in which this teaching is relevant to Christians concerned about the criminal justice system. Often Christians who are working within that system come to the conclusion that their real enemies, are not the criminals or prisoners, but are in fact the officials of the criminal justice system who have a vested interest in its continued survival and operation. Just as it is a temptation for law enforcement officials and the public to think simplistically in terms of criminals as "bad guys" and all others "good", so too it is often a temptation to make the reverse mistake. Since the late 1960's, law enforcement officials and penal authorities have come under increasing attack as the villains of the criminal justice system. They have often been labeled as malicious, evil individuals and the battle-cry "off the pigs" was heard as the left-wing equivalent of "fry the convicts". Yet such type-casting of law enforcement authorities is no more valid or truthful than that of prisoners. The truth is that they, too, are human beings, often very idealistic and motivated human beings, who have been entrusted with the thankless and impossible task of effectively administering an inherently unworkable penal system. Like prisoners, like all human beings, they often do unloving, hateful, evil things. Like prisoners, the cause of such actions on their part is often the inhuman system within which they are caught. While they may be the enemy of the Christian who is seeking the transformation of the criminal justice system, as human beings they are nonetheless deserving of the same love which is due to criminals. Genuine Christian love is therefore not a tool of partisan politics, but a force for the transformation of all human beings. For, the difference between keeper and kept is simply a difference in role. They share a common humanity and a common bondage to the system which, in reality, holds them both (and us) prisoner.

Understood in this way, love can never be the guiding principle for any social system or political institution. For as Emil Brunner observed: "Love is always related to persons, never to things. We can speak of a just law or system, but we cannot speak of a loving law or system."[7] In this we see the real perversion of any attempt to legitimize the criminal justice system as serving "Christian" purposes. For, in the social (as opposed to biblical) sense in which Americans speak of justice:

> . . . justice has to do not with the person (as) person, but with the person in view of "something", a material domain which is not personal . . . Thus in virtue of the idea of justice mankind is placed in an order. He is part of a structure, and it is a structure which orders the whole of life . . . By justice every man is "fitted in", and hence in a way disposed of . . . (justice) severs me from him (others) by drawing round about him a circle into which I may not penetrate, by not admitting me to direct contact with him, himself, since it only shows me what is "his", what "belongs" to him. I have to do, not with him, but with his right.[8]

To the extent that love by its very nature is personal, and unconcerned with social structures, then no "system" of justice can ever be genuinely called Christian. For the realm of justice is one of obligations and rights, and the human person is subordinated to them. This by no means implies that all social efforts to deal with the problem of crime are equally bad; that there is no difference in the degree to which particular institutions are compatible with Christian faith and an ethic of love. It simply means, that to assume a truly Christian understanding on crime can ever be completely represented by inherently impersonal institutions such as courts, criminal codes or prisons, does violence both to the Gospel and to the truth. If Christians are going to bear witness to their faith as it relates to the problem of crime, they must do so individually or as a faith community, without relying upon existing structures either to assist them, or to do so in their stead.

Forgiveness and Reconciliation

The ethic of love which Jesus teaches in the New Testament coincides with one of forgiveness. Jesus said: "Do not judge others, and God will not judge you; do not condemn others, and God will not condemn you; forgive others and God will forgive you." (Luke 6:37) Throughout his ministry Jesus gave forgiveness to sinners who sought it. He chastised, most of all, those who presumed to condemn others. If any element of New Testament faith is relevant for a Christian perspective on criminal justice, certainly it is the teachings on forgiveness.

Popular reaction to any hint of forgiveness for criminals is a telling commentary on American thought on crime. What sparks moral indignation is not a suggestion that we wreak vengeance on criminals, but any suggestion that we forgive them, as in: "You talk like you're actually *forgiving* them for what they've done!"

To seriously consider forgiveness of criminals is really quite alien to American culture. In such a context, talk of forgiveness bears the same air of unreality as does talk of love. Nonetheless, there are valuable insights to be gained by considering the futility of criminal justice from the perspective of Christian forgiveness. Furthermore, to the extent that one wishes to call himself/herself Christian, then certainly it is necessary to ask how Jesus' ethic of forgiveness can be reconciled with American beliefs about crime.

The escalating tide of crime in America, particularly crime which is committed by repeat offenders, is in large part a reflection of an unwillingness to forgive. This unwillingness is demonstrated not just in the imposition of long prison sentences for all varieties of crime, but also in the rejection of ex-offenders by society. As noted in the preceding section, the designation "criminal" is the modern equivalent of the biblical label "unclean". Ex-convicts are routinely shunned by the population at large. Their criminal record marks them for life. Worse still, this social rejection of criminals is often institutionalized via such means as "three-time loser" laws, which impose mandatory life imprisonment or the death sentence on criminals convicted of more than three felonies; or computerized data banks, which provide instant access to an ex-convicts criminal record to police officials, employers, colleges, etc., thereby ensuring that a criminal can never escape from his/her past. One of the most cherished myths of American civil religion, that criminals "pay their debt to society" and then go free, is sheer illusion. One concrete result of this lack of forgiveness for criminals is that they are often inevitably forced back to crime as a matter of both economic and social survival. A life of crime is literally the only life which they are permitted to know.

This lack of forgiveness can be viewed as an escalating spiral of hatred and violence which is continuously fueled by the actions of both participants. People threaten society by committing crimes, often out of the bitterness and despair which results from social oppression. Society, reacting defensively, responds to this threat by subjecting criminals to punishments which confirm their belief that they are being oppressed, and by isolating criminals from the community and its members. But this isolation is only temporary, and criminals, believing even more that they are justified in their bitterness and anger, strike back at society by committing still more crimes. Society, now convinced that criminals are dangerous, indignantly responds with still harsher punishments, which only serves to increase the bitterness of criminals, etc. Thus, hatred breeds only hatred, violence only violence, and a self-perpetuating, inherently destructive cycle is created which makes any reconciliation between community and offender almost impossible. George Jackson, who died in the California prisons as a result of his efforts to resist their dehumanization, recognized this process in his writings. Yet he confessed that even if he ever left prison alive he might be so twisted by the experience that he would be driven to perform violence and hateful actions.[9] Viewed in this perspective, Jesus' teaching that those who do not forgive will not be forgiven has an ironic double meaning. It is not only God but also other human beings who will refuse to forgive those who do not show forgiveness themselves.

Concretely, to show forgiveness for criminals

would involve a willingness to dispense with the question of blame for crime—the perennial debate over whether it is the individual's or society's fault that crime occurs. As it stands now, we are mired in a swamp of self-justification on the part of both society and criminals. Realistically, one can make a persuasive case for both sides of the argument. An ethic of forgiveness would dismiss the very debate itself as irrelevant, thereby moving us beyond the stage of scapegoating to a consideration of the larger task of how to effect a reconciliation between offender and community. For forgiveness by its very nature is oriented toward the future, and does not dwell on the past. Jesus' concern in forgiving sinners was always that they go and sin no more. For an offer of forgiveness to be meaningful, however, we must recognize that releasing people from prison with no resources, with few if any contacts in the community except those whom they met in prison, and with little prospect of finding a place for themselves within the larger society, is not really to forgive, but actually to condemn them to a repetition of their prior experiences with crime. Hence an ethic of forgiveness and the acceptance which it implies must be accompanied by actual acceptance and support from the community, or else it is a false gesture.

It might well be objected that in the New Testament sinners came to Jesus actively seeking forgiveness, but criminals feel no need of forgiveness for their acts. On the surface this appears to be true, for prisoners as a group are not quick to express contrition for their actions. On the contrary, when one first meets a prisoner, he/she is apt to be hostile or withdrawn, and to justify or even lie about the actions which resulted in their imprisonment. Yet as suggested earlier, the gruff manner in which prisoners excuse themselves and their actions obscures the fact that often they are begging pardon for them at the same time. To seek forgiveness requires admitting that one is wrong, thereby exposing oneself to attack and ridicule from all sides. In the struggle for spiritual and psychological survival which takes place in prison, it is absurd to expect that many prisoners would have the strength to risk that vulnerability. Precious few people in the highly religious culture of the Jews were moved to seek forgiveness even in the presence of a man so obviously loving as Jesus. Can we seriously expect prisoners to openly demonstrate contrition in the threatening confines of the penal system?

An ethic of forgiveness for criminals might also be objected to on the grounds that prisoners, in their hostility toward society (a bitterness which is sometimes even directed at people who show concern for them), show an unwillingness both to forgive and to be forgiven. In short, it is argued that criminals are so hardened by their experiences that forgiveness would be wasted on them. But much of this thinking is based on illusion, for criminals are not nearly so vengeful as television scriptwriters would have us believe. In interviews, for instance, they frequently express the opinion that policemen, guards, judges, etc., who are the most obvious and logical targets for their anger, are merely "doing their job". Criminals' hostility is usually impersonal, directed against "society" in the abstract. In this sense they are more forgiving than we are, for their hostility is rooted in despair and resignation in the face of larger social forces, rooted in a sense that they are destined never to belong. Whereas our hostility toward criminals is often far more wilful, rooted in determination not to allow them to belong.

It would once again be naive, however, that a determination to express forgiveness for criminals would result in any immediate transformation of their lives or of the criminal justice system itself. Hence, as with a decision to love, a decision to accept the ethic of forgiveness must be unconditional in that it is made with an awareness of the probability of failure. Likewise it implies a willingness to persist in forgiveness despite the rejection of others. It implies a willingness to forgive not seven times, but "seventy times seven". (Matt. 18:22)

The early Christian communities placed an extraordinary emphasis on forgiveness and reconciliation, and apparently had great success in living up to this standard. Their success was possible, however, because they had a community of shared visions, values and ideals. Reconciliation literally means a *re-*conciliation. It implies that a state of solidarity, a community, existed before, which was then disturbed by an offense against it. In contemporary American society, with its wide diversity, its transient population and its myriad of ethnic, social and economic distinctions, it is difficult to find a real sense of community. Reconciliation is strange to us because the experience of community itself is strange. We have no appreciation for an ideal of restoration of the community because we have so little appreciation for an ideal of community itself. Thus, once again we are led to the conclusion that crime is inseparably linked to the broader question of social relationships between human beings.

Just as an ethic of love cannot possibly be the

guiding principle for a social system of justice, so too an ethic of forgiveness cannot possibly be the basis for a system of law. A wholesale application of "forgiveness" would undermine the very basis of law, which by its very nature insists upon determining liability and requires the existence of sanctions or penalties for enforcing its statutes. This does not mean that forgiveness is irrelevant to the problems of criminal justice. Rather it means that Christians must find a way to express forgiveness personally and through the community, and that they cannot expect political institutions to do so for them.

The Need for Hope

A decision to approach the problem of crime with an ethic of love makes little sense as an isolated act. Certainly such a decision cannot be justified on historical grounds, vindicated by empirical evidence, or described as "rational" in the popular sense of the term. On the contrary, it seems absurd to affirm a belief in love and forgiveness when confronting institutions such as prisons, where powerful cultural myths oppose such thinking; where the institutional processes at work serve to prevent rather than foster human growth; and where the prisoners themselves often come to accept the dehumanizing labels which are pinned to them. There are few easily won victories anywhere in the criminal justice system, and frequently it seems as if no amount of effort, human or divine, will ever succeed in transforming it or those that are trapped within it.

Hence, a decision to accept an ethic of love and forgiveness makes sense only when placed in a broader context, when viewed from the perspective of hope. Hope as it is used here does not mean blind optimism that "tomorrow will be a better day". On the one hand, hope requires an acceptance of the eschatological promise of Jesus that "a society without prisons is a realistic possibility for a redeemed humanity", a belief that "this is the will of God for men".[10] On the other hand, hope consists of a willingness to accept and live in the tension between the not yet realized promise of Jesus, and the still-to-be-transformed institutions of the present. Hope then is a willingness to look beyond what is, to see what might be. While it looks to the future, properly understood hope is not a disinterest in the present. Rather it provides the courage, the inspiration to continue struggling *in* the present to transform the existing order, and thus bring into being the "new order" which typifies a Christian view of the future.

Patrick Kerans has suggested that it is precisely the failure to hope which gives rise to much of the demonic in human history.

> The temptation is to give up hope, to cease to put the future together by putting myself together now. Short-term goals come to define my horizon; selfish considerations predominate . . . How can I bother with long-term goals, with overall considerations, with the coherence of history? . . . And thus human evil emerges. For this is not a simple choice among competing options. This is a decision against being human in its fullness.[11]

A decision to embrace an ethic of love and forgiveness for criminal justice is a decision to take the long-view. It is a decision to reject being imprisoned by the present, and to accept the challenge of "actualizing", of making concrete, of living in the freedom revealed by Jesus. This decision is not something terribly rational, perfectly obvious, or easily defensible. Quite simply, it is an act of faith.

7
HUMAN FREEDOM & SIN

The subjects of sin and human freedom are inextricably connected with all Christian thinking on criminal justice. Historically, the level of Christian interest in these two topics was probably at its highest during the period of heavy Church involvement in the organization of society and the administration of law in the Middle Ages. Medieval scholastic theology, which emphasized the rationality of human beings, developed the principle that, by definition, human action was the product of deliberation; a free exercise of the will. Such a conceptualization easily dove-tailed with church and later civil legal doctrines such as culpability, motive, intent, "premeditation", etc. Consequently, human freedom often came to be viewed as something negative in character. Freedom was viewed as significant, not because it was the creative power by which human beings defined themselves and grew, but because the existence of freedom allowed human beings to resist the laws of men and God, and made them liable for punishment. At the same time, the Church's concern with forging a link between the concept of crime and sin led it to emphasize "sin" as sins, i.e., individual actions. Sin came to be specifically defined as intentional, willful actions taken against the law of God. This was often erroneously interpreted in popular usage as meaning that an individual could avoid sin by not committing sinful actions. Since sin, understood in this way, always involved an intentional act of the will, sinners (and by extension criminals) were viewed as malicious, purposefully evil people who had abused their freedom.

These interpretations of freedom and sin ultimately led to a number of problems in both penology and Christian theology. Much Christian theology and penal ideology have been based upon the assumption that virtually every human action is a free, intentional choice; an exercise of the will. This assumption produced a highly individualistic conception of morality, which holds the individual solely responsible for his/her actions. Social and psychological forces are not accepted as playing a determinative role in the decision-making process. Even if such forces exert pressure on the individual, it is claimed, free will makes it possible for the individual to resist such pressures and in spite of them to make the proper choice.

This rigid stance on free will, adapted from Christian theology by penal ideology, stands at the root of our individualistic thinking about crime. It is what permits us to vigorously punish individual criminals while ignoring larger social forces behind crime, and is the basis for retribution and deterrence theory. Yet this hard line thinking on the subject of free will makes a basic error in logic; namely, it assumes that because every human being has the capacity for freedom (and free choice), that this capacity is realized (and utilized) in every situation. As Raymond-Saleilles argued:

A man fires a gun at another; we know that to fire or not to fire are like possibilities. We conclude that the murderer was well able to realize the alternatives, to act or to refrain. If we believe to have thereby proven the argument that he was as free to act in the one way as to the other, and thus to have established the freedom of his will, we are relying upon an argument that is clearly falacious. The fallacy consists in substituting a general and abstract situation, (the overall existence of human freedom) for a specific and concrete one.[1]

One of the significant truths about human freedom is that it not only involves "the power to anticipate one course or another . . . but in particular it involves consciousness of one's freedom".[2] In other words, to a great extent, one is free only to the extent that one believes himself/herself to be free. Human freedom is real only for the individual who recognizes and affirms its existence. Applied to the subject of crime, this insight is highly relevant. For the simple truth is that most prisoners do not see themselves as free. Rather, they see themselves as victims, as "billiard balls" at the mercy of various psychological and social forces which are beyond their control. It is not so much that they *want* to commit crime, as a strict interpretation of free will insists, as that for various reasons they believe (accurately or not) that they *have* to, that they are forced to. Much of their perception of themselves as being oppressed stems from a belief that they are being held liable for actions which they do not believe they can control. The regimen of prison life, rather than encouraging the use of freedom and fostering responsibility, makes convicts dependent on authorities for their every need, and the capricious use of authority in prisons enforces prisoners' belief that what happens in their lives is indeed beyond their control. Ironically, imprisonment, by brutalizing criminals, ultimately decreases the power to resist evil implied by the concept of free will. Speaking of repeat offenders, Saleilles wrote, "The power to resist (evil) implies the thought of resistance. But the thought of such resistance is not even present. It has been deadened by habit and lost in the growing degeneracy of the man. The more perverted and hardened a man becomes, the less is any freedom of action perceptible in what he does; and hence he becomes less free and less accountable."[3]

Gradually, as a result of various cultural forces, a belief in human freedom has come to be identified with a belief in stiff punishment for crime. To embrace one, a person is commonly expected to embrace the other. Penal ideologists promoted the absurd proposition: if we accept the existence of human freedom, it then follows that we must punish criminals. They then compounded their error by advancing the equally preposterous argument: to refuse to punish criminals is to deny the existence of human freedom.

The inevitable result of this merger of the idea of freedom with the punitive ethic typified by the American penal system was to give human freedom a bad name. To oppose the punitive ethic of American penology, the traditional liberal stance on crime has been that criminals are not free, but totally at the mercy of social and psychological forces, which in turn has fueled the treatment ideal within the penal system. Yet, the treatment model itself is ultimately dehumanizing, and in practice, causes as much or more damage to human lives as do methods of punishment. In another of the ironies of American penal history, the only possibility liberals could see to "humanize" prisons was to deny human freedom and responsibility and to embrace the inherently dehumanizing view of individuals which treatment ideology represents. So we are mired in the midst of either/or thinking: either we accept the existence of human freedom and subject criminals to brutalizing "punishment", or we reject the existence of human freedom and subject criminals to dehumanizing "treatment".

In practical terms, the debate has little significance, for most Americans simply don't care on what grounds criminals are locked away, just so long as a percentage of them *are* locked away and the illusion is fostered that justice is being served and the public order rendered secure. With respect to the life of the Church, however, the issue is of great importance, for belief in human freedom is a central element in most Christian teaching. First, it is becoming more and more apparent to Christian theologians that doctrinaire stances on freedom of the will fail to adequately represent reality, and that the Church needs to become more discerning in its teaching on the dynamics of human freedom. Certainly this will influence Christian thought on crime. More importantly, the debate over freedom and determinism has great significance for the Church's pastoral ministry to prisoners. Prison chaplains are caught in the middle of classical theological teachings on the role of freedom in human decision-making, prisoners' self-perceptions, and the growing body of evidence that crime is strongly influenced if not caused by social and economic forces originating outside of the individual. Chaplains who try to resolve this tension by resorting to a hard-line traditionalist stance on free will are apt to be uneasy with its failure to take account of communal responsibility for crime, and they are likely to be dismissed by the prisoners as being out of touch with reality. On the other hand, chaplains who accept deterministic explanations for crime may well lose sight of their purpose as ministers and perform a function indistinguishable from members of the "treatment" staff. Or they are likely to find that by resorting to deterministic explanations for crime that they are of no help to the prisoners because they thereby encourage their dependence, their lack of freedom, and fail to point the "way" toward individual transformation.

The church should not try to solve the dilemmas of penal ideology; it should ignore them. Within the confines of penal ideology, freedom is conceived of in a limiting, negative way and there is little likelihood that a genuinely Christian appreciation of freedom could emerge. How then can Christians show awareness and concern over the social roots of crime without denying freedom? The solution to this dilemma lies in greater appreciation of the difference between human potential for freedom, and the actual realization of that freedom in a given situation. It is not contradictory for Christians both to recognize the role of social forces in causing crime, and, at the same time, to pursue a vigorous pastoral ministry which extends to individual prisoners an invitation to responsibly exercise human freedom. For a Christian view of freedom does not look backwards to assign blame for previous actions. Rather, it is future-oriented, calling people to a fully human life in the present. The church can be prophetic, criticizing social injustice, without abandoning its teaching on freedom, so long as it is willing to concede that freedom is far more complex than medieval theology has led us to believe and that not all individuals are acting freely in every situation, though they may have the *capacity* to do so.

Hence, in its pastoral ministry, the Church need not primarily concern itself over whether individual prisoners were "truly free" in making particular decisions in the past, or concern itself with being guardian of the "moral order". It can better pursue its mission by encouraging prisoners to make decisions about their future and thereby begin assuming responsibility for their lives in the present.

In addition to re-thinking the question of human freedom as it relates to criminal justice, Christians are also faced with the task of reconsidering the implications of the concept of sin. As noted above, Christians have often tended to interpret sin in a legalistic way—as sins—isolated, willful acts committed by individuals who abuse their freedom in opposition to God's law. This quite limited and narrow understanding of sin greatly influenced the development of western criminal law and is at the root of many Christians' misconceptions about the problem of crime. Therefore, an attempt to formulate a truly Christian approach to the problem of criminal justice must necessarily consider the relationship between the social reality of crime and the theological concept of sin.

One of the chief manifestations of the emphasis on individualism in conceiving of sin is the ascetical tradition of the Church. As Gregory Baum describes it:

> In the ascetical tradition of the Christian Church, the power in man which makes him sin, which makes him go against the divine and human orders, which makes him do all kinds of crazy, harmful and vicious things, is self-aggrandize-

ment. Man sins because he loves himself exces-
sively. He wants to put himself into the center
of his universe; he wants to build his own kingdom, he becomes a law unto himself . . . (he)
is willing to interfere with the lives of others and
resent, even revolt against, the kingdom of God.
Man sins because he loves himself too much.[4]

Based on this tradition, the remedies for sin become
"self-abnegation, self-effacement, humility, obedience
. . ."[5] It is not difficult to see how such an understanding of sin gave rise to institutions such as the monastic
prison.

On a pastoral level, this conception of sin has
often led prison chaplains to focus their efforts upon
evoking from prisoners expressions of repentance and
humility. Many chaplains see it as a critical first step
that a criminal admit he/she is wrong, that he/she evidence humility and a willingness to submit to law and
authority. If only the prisoner would cease to revolt
against the established order of things, then it would be
possible to effect some transformation in him/her.
Some chaplains are anxious to provide rules for governing behavior in order to aid the prisoner in learning
how to live a "moral" life.

However, there is a significant problem with this
understanding of sin. For sin, as it is defined in
scripture, is far more then self-centeredness and self-
love. As Baum points out, theologically "sin is defined
as the rejection of God's love".[6] This rejection is not
always, nor even usually, based upon excessive self-
love. More often than not, particularly in the case of
prisoners, it is caused by an inability to accept oneself,
by an excessive self-hatred. We know from modern

psychology that many human actions are motivated from a deep mistrust of, and dislike for, oneself. Destructive actions, directed toward both the self and others, are often reflections of this self-hatred. People do hateful things usually because they have not experienced love, and one facet of the love which they lack involves a healthy appreciation of self.

Most people in prison have been subjected to a life of rejection and isolation. They have experienced precious little love in the world. Their criminal acts are usually destructive of themselves, both in obvious physical ways (drug usage and prostitution), and in more subtle spiritual and psychological ways (the guilt and self-condemnation which follows upon acts of violence). But criminals' hostility toward others often obscures this lack of self-appreciation and self-love, which is ultimately behind that hostility. A colleague of mine once listened to a prisoner condemn society and other people for several minutes, emphasizing how much he hated both. He was then interrupted and perceptively asked, "And how much do you hate yourself?", at which the prisoner looked away and responded, "Don't even ask me that, man." Self-rejection by prisoners is tied to other themes in their life such as despair and the tendency to view life as being beyond their control. It is frequently manifested by prisoners saying to chaplains or others interested in their life, "it's no use", and "why do you waste your time on someone like me?"

This is an important consideration in the way in which we approach crime. Currently the penal methods which we employ serve to dehumanize, degrade, and thereby increase the rejection which prisoners have for self. Likewise in the pastoral ministry to prisoners, prisoners' rejection of overtures by chaplains is often ascribed to self-centeredness and pride, when, in reality, at the root of it is self-hatred and despair. Focusing on the superficial aspects of morality, such as isolated instances of behavior and obedience to rules, will only serve to obscure the far more significant aspects of a prisoner's struggle with life, including the struggle to find and maintain a viable sense of self. Chaplains who view their mission exclusively in terms of persuading prisoners not to commit further criminal acts, in terms of preventing the further "commission of sins", are apt to miss the forest for the trees; for, the various isolated destructive actions of prisoners are merely manifestations of the existence of a larger state of sin—the absence of love in their lives. Moreover, chaplains who continually berate prisoners for their lives and bombard them with rules by which to live, serve only to deepen self-hatred and consequently increase criminals' animosity toward other human beings as well. In short, a judgmental ministry to prisoners is not only ineffective in speaking to their real problems, but is likely to do more harm than good.

Still, it does not then follow that the simple key to effecting a transformation in prisoners' lives lies in conveying to them, making real for them, the experience of Christian love. The problem is more complex than that. For, as Baum goes on to say, "man's sin is connected with his unwillingness to believe that God is good and to receive the gifts that make him free. Man resists God's love not only because he is selfish but also, and perhaps even primarily, because he cannot trust and be open to the goodness that is available in life".[7] Hence, the rejection of love, both human and divine, stems not just from a failure to experience it, but from the failure to believe in the possibility of its existence as well. Prisoners' cynicism about others and about themselves is a manifestation of this. Many prisoners simply do not believe that they can experience a transformation in themselves and the way in which they see life. To many, talk of a "new being" is simply false hope. From the standpoint of penal ideology, this would be another justification for keeping them isolated from the population at large on the grounds that they are incorrigible. From the standpoint of Christian faith, this is a description of the challenge which faces Christians who wish to work in prisons.

Individualistic conceptions of sin have also erroneously led us to believe that sin is something rather easily vanquished. One can conquer sin by resolving not to "commit sins" again. Parallel beliefs underlie the criminal justice system, where we assume that what is needed to prevent future crime is a simple act of good will by the prisoner, who resolves not to commit crimes again. Accordingly we are outraged at repeat offenders, because we interpret their continued criminality as a sign of their malice and unwillingness to live peacefully with the rest of the community. Yet this surprise and outrage over repeat offenders might not be so prevalent if we had as keen a sense of the pervasive power of sin as the early Christians. For, as Paul wrote, despite good intentions, sin exercises a power over human lives which can overwhelm conscious attempts to conquer it.

For even though the desire to do good is in me, I am not able to do it. I don't do the good I want to do; instead, I do the evil that I do not want to do.

If I do what I don't want to do, this means that no longer am I the one who does it; instead, it is the sin that lives in me. My inner being delights in the law of God. But I see a different law at work in my body—a law that fights against the law my mind approves of. It makes me a prisoner to the law of sin which is at work in my body. (Romans 7:18-23)

Among prisoners, contrary to popular belief, good intentions are the rule rather than the exception. Most people in prison, for whatever reasons, have at least some resolve not to commit crimes again. Yet regardless of how strong such resolve may be, they often find themselves drawn almost irresistibly to doing things which ultimately result in their being sent back to prison. Doubtlessly, in the case of drug addicts, the power of compulsion stems largely from physical dependence upon narcotics. But behind such a physical dependency there lies even deeper human tendencies and problems which at times seemingly compel individuals toward following undesirable paths in their lives. Beyond mere force of habit, there exists in the lives of all human beings (despite their better judgment and good intentions) the inclination to follow certain courses of action which prove to be destructive of themselves and others.

Sin, then, is more than simply the intentional abuse of human freedom. It is the existence of "unfreedom". Human beings can literally be trapped into certain patterns in their lives which they may resist and wish to overcome and still be unable to control. Thus Paul could conclude: "We are not fighting against human beings, but against the wicked spiritual forces in the heavenly world, the rulers, authorities, and cosmic powers of this dark age." (Ephesians 6:12) In other words, beyond the conscious efforts of human beings, there are suprapersonal forces (not necessarily demons per se); spiritual forces such as hatred, despair, self-rejection, among others which can trap and imprison human beings. These forces are larger than any one individual, and cannot always be resisted by an individual's good intentions.

This is certainly a significant insight, because penal ideology asserts that to avoid committing crime requires nothing more than a simple act of the will. From the standpoint of Christian theology, this is a dubious assumption at best. On a practical level, anyone who has worked with prisoners for a long period knows that the problem is far more complex. The frustrating experience of seeing prisoners try and still fail becomes more comprehensible when viewed from the perspective of Christian teaching on sin. For, what Paul implies is that it is possible to attempt to break out of old life patterns only to fail and be immersed in them still. Many individuals who work with prisoners expect that they will see great transformation in their lives in a short period of time. While sometimes this happens, more often the opposite is the case, and little apparent change is seen. It is then a temptation to quit the struggle, to conclude that all of the various myths about prisoners being intractable and evil are true. Only after recognizing the deeper forces at work in human beings does it make sense to continue in spite of apparent failure.

Part of the inability to comprehend the pervasiveness and complexity of sin is the result of an inability to recognize the existence of sin as a fundamental element in all human endeavor. The "principalities and powers" referred to by Paul do not just affect individual human beings. They affect human systems and institutions as much if not more. As John Swomley of Missouri's St. Paul School of Theology pointed out:

(Paul) . . . did not view men simply as separate entities who yield to specific sins and vices but instead saw that men inherited certain structures of existence. These structures may originally have had the good purpose of holding life together, in much the same way as law serves a useful purpose but can be perverted into an instrument of oppression.[8]

When human beings become part of certain social systems, they lose their identity as people, and both perpetrate and suffer from actions which are caused by the basic sinfulness of those systems.[9] In the American penal system, some individuals, as part of their official role as "keeper" within the system, do things which dehumanize and brutalize other human beings. Yet, these destructive actions are not considered sinful for they are undertaken for good purposes, and the individuals who administer the penal system do not conceive of themselves as having evil intentions. At the same time, the prisoners who are at the mercy of the mechanisms of the penal system are often led to do equally destructive things in acting out their role as the "kept". But we blame this on the prisoners, whom we believe are evil, and fail to see the forces at work which led them to do such things in the first place.

Prisons by their very nature are institutions which create an unnatural state of human affairs. One group of human beings holds virtually unchecked power over another. Human beings are kept confined in debilitating physical conditions. Normal human relationships are strained and distorted. Contacts with the "real world" and with those people whom the prisoner considers precious in life are severed. Conclusive proof of this was provided by a 1972 experiment at Stanford University, which created a mock prison to test how various individuals would respond to the roles which they were asked to play.[10] All participants were college students or professors, and extreme personality types were excluded from the experiment. After only six days (out of a projected fourteen) the experiment had to be stopped because all of those involved, both the keepers and kept, were suffering severe psychological side-effects. This was simply an experiment, conducted by reasonable, well-educated people who knew that it was only an experiment. It did not even begin to approach the reality of imprisonment as it is known by thousands of human beings in America every day. And yet we believe that such institutions will not serve the purposes of evil, but rather foster the services of good?

A final problem with popular Christian thinking on sin, as it relates to the subject of criminal justice, is the tendency of Christians to overlook the communal nature of sin. In our haste to label others as criminals, as sinners, we often overlook the fact that we ourselves are by no means the righteous. The myth of the creation does not just imply that we have a common heritage as children of God, it also implies that we, as human beings, share a common heritage of sin. Criminals are not so very different from us as we would like to believe. They simply manifest their sinfulness in such a manner as to bring attention from civil authorities. As Bruce Jackson puts it:

We often read or talk about the *criminal* as if this were some homogeneous category, as if the word defined a personality type. It is no more useful than the word "killer", which could, given the proper circumstances, cover any of us.[11]

This same sentiment was expressed by Oscar Wilde in his "The Ballad of Reading Gaol".

Yet each man kills the thing he loves,
By each let this be heard,
Some do it with a bitter look,
Some with a flattering word,
The coward does it with a kiss,
The brave man with a sword.[12]

Moreover, criminals are often motivated by the same kinds of destructive impulses which propel American society as a whole. As noted earlier, criminals often share the values and outlook of the larger society, although they do not see themselves as a part of it. Their criminality, to a certain extent, is the result of their attempt to pursue the great "American dream" of the easy life, via illegitimate means. For as Robert K. Merton pointed out: "Recourse to legitimate channels for 'getting in the money' is limited by a class structure . . . Despite our persisting open-class ideology, advance toward the success goals is relatively rare and notably difficult for those armed with little formal education and few economic resources."[13] People limited in this way often turn to crime. Thus, the motivation of non-criminals is in many cases just as self-seeking as that of the criminal. The non-criminal simply has more means with which to pursue material goals within the framework of accepted society. From a Christian perspective, the frantic "rush to get in the money" is equally pointless and sinful, whether one does it by resorting to petty street crime, or by engaging in dubious business practices which unfairly exploit competitors and consumers. We are so concerned with the particulars of crime that we completely overlook the destructive materialistic values of the society at large which much crime reflects. In many cases a criminal's "problem" is not so much that he/she has committed an illegal act, but that he/she has placed undue emphasis on obtaining material goods, such as money and the social status which accompanies the possession of it. Stripped of cultural differences, both the ambitious Wall Street lawyer and the street corner pimp are engaged in a self-destructive quest to be thought of as a "big man".

As noted earlier, one reason why we can treat criminals so brutally is because we see them as different from ourselves, as fundamentally non-human. Consequently, it is vitally important to recognize that every human being is sinful, and the fact that we manifest our sinfulness in more or less obvious ways makes us no more or less worthy in the eyes of God. For as long as we insist upon drawing a simplistic distinction between the sinner (the criminal) and the saved (the rest of us), then it will be easy to justify the atrocities which are committed against criminals.

Frequently people will refer to crimes as "inhuman acts". In fact, given the inherent sinfulness of all human beings, the opposite is true. Nothing could be more human than crime. Human beings will always fail, and inevitably the community must deal with that failure. Outrage over crime is partly frustration over our own fallen humanity.

But Christian teaching has not just emphasized that all human beings are sinful. It has also recognized that as a community we are all responsible for sin. Sinful acts by individuals obviously have an effect upon the life of the community. Beyond that, however, sinful actions such as crime are a reflection of the life of the community. For the failings of an individual member of the community often signify that this person's needs are not being met. When crime occurs, it is usually as much because society has failed as it is because the individual has failed. As Harvey expressed it:

> . . . every time one citizen invokes the use of force to restrain or dissuade a fellow citizen from a criminal course of action or to punish him for a crime—on every such occasion the heart of the sensitive Christian must wince: a man—each of us—has failed to attain that depth of love which is revealed to us in Christ and which has the power to reach the heart of every human being.[14]

As Paul Tillich maintained, each individual is responsible for contributing to the destiny of the community of which he/she is a part.[15] Our toleration of the many social structures and pressures of modern life, which are at the root of crime, implicates us in the criminal act. Theologically (as opposed to legally) speaking, there are no "innocent" victims of crime. If we take Christianity seriously, then in fact, all of us share responsibility for what our brothers and sisters do.

8
THE CHRISTIAN WITNESS RECONSIDERED: "TO PRISONERS . . . FREEDOM"

Christianity is a religion which holds a promise of salvation for human beings. Through Jesus Christ, Christians believe that humankind is redeemed. The salvific character of Christianity is often overlooked in topical theological writing, yet truly we cannot take a Christian approach to any problem without finally asking: how is the Christian promise of salvation relevant?

We need not approach the question blindly, for specific attention is paid to the situation of imprisonment within scripture. The term prison, of course, as it appears in the bible, is not the exact equivalent of the term as it is used today. Typically, prisons in biblical times held political prisoners, not criminal convicts, as crime was punished by means other than imprisonment. In general, the bible viewed prisoners as the victims of social oppression, unfortunate people who suffered because of the general sinfulness of humankind. Still, this description is not so inappropriate when one considers the inhabitants of contemporary American prisons, and certainly is of some relevance to Christian attitudes toward prisoners.

The redemptive promise of freedom to prisoners first appeared in the Old Testament book of Isaiah which is now frequently interpreted by Christian theologians as a foreshadowing of the coming of the Christ. Isaiah's prophecies are referred to as the messianic promise.

> The spirit of the Lord God is upon me, because the Lord has annointed me; He has sent me to bring glad tidings to the lowly, to heal the broken-hearted, to proclaim liberty to the captives and release to the prisoners.
>
> (Isaiah 61:1)

In the New Testament, Jesus names visiting prisoners as one of the specific ministries for his followers (Matt. 25:31ff.). Paul, in his letters, later describes Jesus as having fulfilled the messianic promise, as having brought freedom to prisoners (Heb. 10:34; 13:3). Thus, from a biblical perspective, salvation as it relates to prisons is inextricably connected with the problem of freedom.

But we must determine how this promise of freedom is to be understood. Contrary to the views of some writers, it is wrong to interpret this promise of freedom literally, as referring to the physical liberty of prisoners.[1] For Jesus did not lead a political revolution, capturing prisons and opening their gates. In the light of recent theological development, notably some branches of "liberation theology" it is a temptation to conclude that we should interpret the promise of freedom literally, to conclude that freedom is meaningful only in a physical sense. Yet to accept such an approach is to do violence to the Gospel, in which Jesus *proclaimed* a new state of being, not dependent upon political power. Freedom in the biblical sense then is not necessarily physical freedom.

This does not mean that Christians should not worry about political and social situations, or that we should not be concerned with the physical reality of imprisonment. It merely means that our concern is a *qualified* concern, one which points to something deeper than the immediate physical situation in which we happen to find ourselves. Some prison chaplains spend so much time trying to alleviate the dreadful physical conditions of prisons, by doing favors and running errands for prisoners, that they are prevented from turning their attention to more significant problems which lie beneath the grim exteriors of imprisonment. A chaplain, or any Christian who works toward the transformation of the penal system can serve as little more than another social worker on the staff, whose services the state is only too glad to accept, especially since such efforts help to ease tensions within the prison and relieve the state of its responsibility for providing humane care for prisoners. Christian attempts to alleviate the immediate suffering which prisons cause must necessarily be *symbols* of concern which are linked to a broader concern for a more significant liberation of criminals.

What then is this deeper liberation with which Christians are concerned? In traditional theological language, the liberation which is promised by Christianity is liberation from the powers of sin and death which was won by the sacrifice of Jesus. Typically, it has been assumed that if this promise of freedom is not to be taken literally, then it must be interpreted in some supra-historical way—Jesus frees us "in the hereafter" or "the next world"; we are liberated at death, when we escape the fires of hell and attain eternal life. Yet salvation, understood in this way, has seemingly little relevance for the now, the present. It merely refers to some future happening. Certainly such a concept of salvation has little relevance for prisoners, who must deal with the difficulties of "getting over" from day to day. Moreover, it tempts us to refuse to take seriously the world around us, human life and human history, for all of that will pass away. The sometimes disastrous consequences of this strict other-worldly approach to Christianity have been amply demonstrated. Likewise we have seen that scripture, properly understood, insists upon just the opposite, and requires that Christians face life with seriousness now. If we maintain that Christian faith *is* relevant to the problems of criminal justice, then it is necessary to give some concrete form to the promise of salvation in the lives of prisoners and others, lest it seem that talk of such liberation is merely indulgence in self-delusion. The remainder of this chapter focuses on how the salvific promise of freedom is specifically meaningful in coming to grips with the problems of criminal justice.

Freedom to Criminals

The promise of freedom proclaimed by Jesus is directed first to those who are (literally) prisoners within the American penal system. In spite of physical captivity, the New Testament maintains, it is possible to be free. On the face of it this is surely a strange claim, for there appears to be little real freedom present to one who is held behind bars. Perhaps this promise would make more sense if it were interpreted as: 1) an invitation from God to make a fundamental decision, namely, a decision to choose life over death; and

2) as an invitation to seek liberation from the various manifestations of death which exercise power over human existence.

The invitation to eternal life which Jesus offers, according to the New Testament, does not exclusively refer to some future state of being. As Paul Tillich points out: "Eternal life is not continuation of life after death. Eternal life is beyond past, present and future: we come from it, we live in its presence, we return to it. It is never absent—it is the divine life in which we are rooted and in which we are destined to participate in freedom . . ."[2] Jesus calls human beings to be liberated by embracing eternal life now.

In the context of the prison, a decision to accept this challenge first would be a decision to *resist* the power of death which prisons represent. For if anything is clear about prisons, it is that they are institutions which are destructive of the human person, institutions which are opposed to life. A decision to accept the way of life over the way of death could be manifested in many specific ways. It could be manifested in the refusal to act out the role of conniving, ruthless "criminal" or "con" which prisoners are expected to fall into. It could be evidenced by resistance to attempts to dehumanize, from both prison officials and fellow prisoners, which are so characteristic of American prisons. It could mean resistance to the various attempts to manipulate one's personality via the coercive means of treatment. It could take the form of purposeful resistance to the penal system through the courts and the media. Any rejection of the hatred and despair which are embodied in American prisons, any affirmation of the human dignity of those held in prison could be an active demonstration of a refusal to yield to the power of death. As Christian theologian William Stringfellow concluded, in a situation where the power of death becomes institutionalized, it is only by resistance to that power that one can find life.[3]

The courage to resist the powers of death, however, is only one facet of genuine Christian liberation. Christian liberation is also a liberation from the various spiritual powers which oppress human beings, effecting a spiritual change which influences one's perspective on all reality. In short, it offers a spiritual new being. As has been emphasized throughout this study, the spiritual maladies which oppress prisoners are just as critical in their lives as are the various social conditions which affect them. Prisoners' self-hatred, their guilt, their inability to love and be loved, their purposelessness and despair—all of these essentially represent unmet spiritual needs. The ultimate causes of crime are spiritual, not psychological or social, and for as long as we fail to recognize this we will be unable to speak to the basic problems of those we call criminals.

Salvation to the prisoner would consist of his/her finding the means to put together the various pieces of his/her broken life. There are many sources of healing in the world, but to the Christian, the key lies in the person of Jesus, who relieves us of guilt; gives us a purpose; shows us a way. Christian faith is God's gift to humankind, his revelation of himself which shows us a way of making sense out of the immediate life situation in which we find ourselves. Tragically, Christian faith has not been a gift to many Americans, and seldom has it been a gift to those in prison. Sometimes it has been an instrument of further repression. The promise of salvation through Jesus appears to be widely unfulfilled. And yet, if Jesus were alive today, one suspects that if he taught anywhere he would teach in the prisons.

The resolution of this problem is suggested by the very words of this last sentence—"if Jesus were alive today". The simple truth is that if Jesus is *not* alive today, it is because we as his followers have failed to find him present. There is little liberation and healing in prisons because there has been little effort to effect such liberation on the part of the vast majority of Christians.

> There are innumerable degrees and kinds of saving grace . . . But if we call him (Jesus) the savior we must remember that *God* is the savior *through* him and that there are a host of liberators and healers, including ourselves, through whom the divine salvation works in all mankind.[4]

This is not to deny that God is the source of salvation. It is merely to say that we have failed to take seriously our duty as Christians to "go and teach all nations". In Carlo Carretto's analogy: "We are the wire, God is the current. Our only power is to let the current pass through us. Of course, we have the power to interrupt it and say 'no'. But nothing more."[5] We have assumed that grace is some mysterious force which operates independently of human life, and that salvation is something which has been settled permanently by Jesus' life and death. Perhaps we assume that if God has plans for prisoners, that *he* will implement them. (This was one of the fundamental premises of the penitentiary system—isolate convicts so that God's saving grace could work upon them without other distractions.) Today the American penal system is designed to implement the plans which certain human beings (those in power) have for other human beings (those without power). As Christians, our task is to discern and then to follow (as best we can) the will of God for both.

If there is to be any liberation in prisons it will require an aggressive Christian ministry there. All too often Christian ministry to prisons has been passive. A chaplain is assigned to a jail or prison, and he defines his role as performing religious services for whomever requests them. It is assumed, however, that he is responsible only for those prisoners who are members of his congregation, or are interested in joining it.[6] Often there is little attempt to engage prisoners who do not first approach the minister. For as long as this constitutes the Christian ministry in prison, little true Christian liberation will occur among prisoners. Likewise, for as long as Christian ministry is a verbal ministry, one which is not supported by actions which vindicate promises of liberation, then prisoners will remain skeptical of Christianity. This does not simply mean that ministers must practice what they preach. It means that the Christian community must live what it supposedly represents. It means that the Christian ministry to prisons is not a clerical ministry alone—it is a lay ministry as well. All Christians must involve themselves in the struggle to liberate those in prison. It is meaningless for chaplains to preach reconciliation if a prisoner is released to find that he has no place in the community. Christians must join their ministers in working with those in prison, both in attending to those in prison and in aiding them upon release. Truly the problem is that the harvest is plenty but the workers are few.

There are several apparent objections to the above. First, it could be said that prisoners won't respond to the best-intentioned efforts, that talk of liberation and salvation with respect to prisoners is ridiculous. Certainly it is true that not everyone wishes to be saved. Again one of Paul Tillich's sermons expresses it best: "We may prefer disease to health, enslavement to liberty. There are many reasons for the desire not to be healed, not to be liberated. He who is weak can exercise a power over his environment, over his family and friends, which can destroy trust and love but which gives satisfaction to him who exercises this power through weakness."[7] However, as was the case with attempting to express love and forgiveness for prisoners, we must recognize that the attempt to liberate prisoners carries with it no guarantee of success. If it did, it would not require an act of faith at all to follow Jesus, it would merely be common sense. But we are informed that God's wisdom is not human wisdom. If it appears ridiculous to try to liberate prisoners, in light of the New Testament, perhaps that is all the more reason for trying to do so.

It might also be objected that having spent the better part of this study attacking prisons, that it is completely inconsistent to imply that they can be the instruments of liberation. This is certainly a difficult objection, because in fact prisons by themselves cannot be instruments of liberation. Liberation must take place *in spite of* them. For while we may wish there were no prisons, there are, and there will continue to be for quite some time. And if we maintain that we, ourselves and prisoners, are helpless when faced with the reality of prisons, then we have said that the Gospel is irrelevant, and that the liberation promised by

Jesus is dependent upon political and social events. What's more, we have condemned prisoners to a hopeless existence of waiting for a revolution which probably will not come in their lifetime. The fact that prisons are not the cause of any genuine human liberation must not blind us to the fact that liberation needs to continue, regardless of the particular social context.

Frequently, pity for prisoners and concern over physical conditions in prison masks a subtle dehumanization of prisoners. In saying that prisoners cannot rise above the penal system, implicitly we are saying that they are less than fully human. While Christians are right to decry the conditions of prisons, underestimating the human potential of prisoners for freedom in the face of injustice belittles them no less than treatment theory does.

Finally, it might be objected that whereas much of the emphasis of this study has been upon the way in which society is responsible for crime, in this chapter, the emphasis is placed upon dealing with individual prisoners. This last objection leads into the next aspect of liberation which must be considered; namely the liberation of people who are not criminals, but are in a very real way prisoners nonetheless.

Freedom to Non-criminals

In his letter to the Hebrews, Paul admonishes Christians not to forget people in prison. Frequently the verse in which he does so is translated something like: "Remember those who are in prison, as though you were in prison with them." (Hebrews 13:3) This translation seems sensible, for it appears that Paul is merely extending the Great Commandment ("do unto others . . .") to the situation of prisons. But a more literal translation of the original Greek text expresses a profound social and theological insight. In the original Greek, Paul's words read: "Remember those in prison, for you are prisoners with them yourselves."[8] In other words, people who are not physically held prisoner are prisoners all the same, and are as much in need of liberation as those actually in prison. The physical confinement of criminals signals a need for society's liberation, not just the liberation of individual criminals.

We are responsible for the suffering of those in prison because ostensibly it is on our behalf that prisons exist. All of the officials of the criminal justice system are surrogates for us—legislators, police, prosecutors, judges, jailors—all of them justify their actions as being for the protection of the community to which we belong. Even officials who are uncomfortable with their roles deny responsibility for what they do. "I'm just doing my job. It's not up to me to set policy." Ultimately, all of the practices of our criminal justice system are referred back to the will of "the people". We are responsible for the failure of those in prison because we participate in and benefit from the broader social structures which are at the root of crime. Finally, we are responsible for failing to look beyond social, cultural myths to see the people who are hidden by the mask of criminality and isolated by the walls of prison.

All of this suggests that we, ourselves, as individuals and as a community of believers, are not yet liberated. We deny our brotherhood and sisterhood with those in prison, we deny our relatedness to their life—and in so doing repudiate our unity with the source of life itself. We cannot yet love as Jesus loved, and so we too are not yet saved. In such a context, the words of frequently imprisoned American labor organizer Eugene V. Debs begin to make sense: "While there is a soul in prison, I am not free."

Our unconcern does not simply extend to convicts in prison. It extends to prison staff as well. We think nothing of asking them to do the job they do. It does not occur to us that they are dehumanized and imprisoned by the institution as well. In many ways, the custodians of American prisons are even more pathetic than the prisoners, because at least the prisoners are aware of their captivity. The keepers of our prisons, however, from the front-line guards to the architects of "scientific" penology, are usually so trapped in self-righteousness and rationalizations of what they do, that they cannot even see how they often surrender their human identity to the roles which they are asked to play.

Martin Luther King, in his teaching on the problem of racism, maintained that it is necessary to combat social oppression not just for the sake of the oppressed, but that it is equally if not more important to fight oppression for the sake of the oppressor.[9] For it is the oppressor who has the greater spiritual affliction. Similarly, William Stringfellow has claimed that in every act of violence the perpetrator is as much a victim as he/she is an aggressor, because violence dehumanizes whomever engages in it.[10] Thus Christian concern cannot be a limited one. It must extend equally to criminals, guards, fellow human beings and ourselves.

Viewed in this way, Christian involvement in criminal justice is not a "take-it-or-leave-it" proposition. Charity is not at the base of Christian concern over the issues of criminal justice. Rather, if we take seriously the New Testament call for liberation, both our own, and that of all people, then Christian presence in prisons is an absolute necessity.

We have forgotten Paul's warning to the Romans (whose state was to the ancient world what America is to the modern): "Do not conform outwardly to the standards of this world, but let God transform you inwardly by a complete change of your mind." (Romans 12:2) To one who is aware of what penology in America represents, then, the task is resistance, not support. The truth is that penal ideology and Christian belief are deeply incompatible. As a rule Christians have resisted examining this incompatibility, preferring instead to remain within the familiar and secure confines of American civil religion. In reality, American Christians are being faced with moments of decision in many areas where religious belief clashes with cultural myth. This study has attempted to draw the lines of battle; to make Christians aware of *their* imprisonment; to show that one cannot be a Christian and still endorse the practices of penology in America. Hopefully, more and more Christians will find themselves faced with the challenge of living out their belief. As this happens, Christian efforts to transform the practice of criminal justice in America will multiply.

If, however, individual Christians do not find support in this struggle from fellow believers, they find themselves in the midst of an even deeper spiritual struggle, that of finding their identity within a hostile church. Frequently Christians who possess a progressive social consciousness find themselves at odds with their own community of believers. Many prison chaplains and lay Christians in recent years have been renegades within their own Church. If any branch of the pastoral ministry has failed to receive mainstream support, it is criminal justice. Sentiments such as the one's expressed in this study would doubtless be questioned in many quarters of the Church. Hence if Christians are to approach criminal justice from a unified point of view, it is necessary to speak of one final aspect of liberation, namely, the liberation of the Church.

Freedom to the Church

It is widely accepted among Christian Church leaders and theologians that the Church itself is continually in need of renewal. The need for such renewal is nowhere greater than in the area of the Church's mission with respect to criminal justice. Historically, the Church's involvement with criminal justice in America is paradoxical. On the one hand the Church is in many ways responsible for the course which American penology has taken. Early in the American experience it was Christians themselves who were the architects of the criminal law and penal practices, and they relied upon Church tradition and Christian theology for their inspiration. As time went by, although American society became less avowedly Christian, the institutions of the criminal justice system remained quasi-religious institutions, which were steeped in Christian traditions and received the enthusiastic support of organized religion. In recent times, as America has become more of a secular society, Christian support of the criminal justice system has been channeled through Christian theology and participation in American civil religion. In short, despite recent Christian criticisms of the practice of criminal justice in America, there can be no doubt that the Christian churches, both as institutions and as communities of believers, have played a critical role in shaping these institutions into what they are today. If we criticize these institutions, it must be criticism grounded in repentance and remorse, for Christians are by no means free from responsibility for their evolution.

On the other hand, at the same time as Christians have openly or tacitly supported the development of the criminal justice system, the Church has also abrogated responsibility for the development of American penology by largely ignoring the problem from the mid-nineteenth century until quite recently. The secular state has assumed the role of giver and protector of moral values, and the criminal law and penal system are the principal instruments of its control. The Church has uncritically supported the state and penal system, and has just begun to confront the fact that civil religion and Christian religion are at odds on many issues. Christian theologians in particular have contributed to the sanctification of the state by advancing theories which justify governmental authority and power, without due consideration to the dehumanizing institutions to which such theories often lend support.

With respect to Christian theology, many of the problems created could be much alleviated if only Christian theologians would begin to show more interest in socio-political issues. Or, if only they would concern themselves with illuminating "the way", instead of concentrating on saying clever things in many different ways. Likewise Christian theologians could perform a valuable service by clearly distinguishing the Christian meaning and function of terms such as justice, punishment, law, and the common good, in contrast to the ways in which these terms are so often corrupted in common usage.

The larger problem of the Church's relationship to society, however, is much more complex, and far too difficult for this study. Some Christians might long for the "purity" of pre-Constantian Christianity, when the Church was not involved in worldly affairs. But such a wish might lead to a Church composed of a spiritual elite, with little or no involvement in the world. Furthermore, it is absurd to expect that the Church or society can simply overlook hundreds of years of Church involvement in western culture. Other Christians might long for the medieval Church, which truly held sway over the political and social development of the times. But if the middle ages taught the Church anything, it taught it the danger of attempting to exercise temporal power while at the same time remaining true to its mission.

The truth is that we live in a post-Christian society, and the Church in America must come to grips with that fact. Its counsel is not likely to be sought, and not likely to be followed except where it is a means of legitimizing the decisions of those who hold power. The problem, as Jean Danielou plainly expressed it in his *Prayer as a Political Problem*, is "how are society and religion to be joined without either making religion a tool of the secular power or the secular power a tool of religion?"[11] The Church has not yet found the answer to this question, but perhaps more so than any other theological issue, it is critical in determining the future shape of the Church's ministry in criminal justice.

9
FAITH IN ACTION

Books of this kind usually end with a comprehensive series of recommendations which propose the "answer" to the problem under discussion. Authors feel that their work is incomplete or unjustified if they cannot offer the definitive resolution of the issues discussed. Such recommendations are very comforting. They create the illusion that matters are well in hand, and that certain steps, if taken, will remove the weight of responsibility from the community's shoulders. Furthermore, most recommendations tend to distance a problem, because they are almost always aimed at some non-personal entity—"the Church should . . .", "the government should . . ." etc. In some peculiar way, recommendations on social problems hold everyone socially accountable, and thereby no one personally accountable.

If anything is clear from this study, it is that the question of what we do with people who violate the law is not simply a social problem which will be settled once and for all. Crime will always occur, and the attempts to deal with crime will always present a challenge to Christians. The task of Christians is not necessarily to discover how to eradicate crime. Their primary task is to discover how to bear witness to their faith in whatever situation they find themselves.

It is tempting to say that it is not worth the effort;

that nothing can be done until everything is done; that no one can confront crime humanely until everyone is willing to do so. This of course is false, since Christians can always bear witness alone, regardless of whether society chooses to agree.

The following suggested courses of reflection and action are not proposed as social programs to eliminate crime. Rather, they are ways in which individual Christians, or groups of Christians, can discover the relevance of their faith to criminal justice. Likewise, they are possible means of symbolizing and actualizing what we profess to believe as Christians.

Attitudinal Change

The first, and perhaps most crucial task for Christians concerned over crime and justice is to examine their attitudes about crime, criminals, punishment, etc. As with most subjects, our thinking on crime is the product of subtle, conditioning influences of which we may not even be aware. Therefore, we must start by reflecting on how we respond to crime, how we feel criminals ought to be treated, what we think the purposes of the criminal justice system to be, etc. Are we outraged by crime, or by the treatment of criminals? Or perhaps by both?

Next, concentrate on how our views about criminal justice can be reconciled with our understanding of Christianity. As Christians, do we preach forgiveness, only to condemn overtures of forgiveness toward criminals? Do we profess to stand for justice, only to ignore the injustice which permeates our society's response to crime? Where do we get our thinking about criminal justice—from careful reflection upon the many issues it presents, or from the popular press and tv?

As focal points for this reflection, we might consider the following:

—— the meaning of Christianity; its relevance to the issues presented by criminal justice.

—— the humanity of those trapped by the criminal justice system, including prisoners, officials, and ourselves.

—— the possibilities for finding a better way to respond to crime as a society.

—— the way in which we as individuals can help to bring about change, not just in the system itself, but in the lives of individuals affected by it.

While individual Christians can undertake such reflection alone, it would even be better if those in positions of responsibility were to lead them in doing so— whether they be bishops, pastors, ministers, lay leaders, teachers, etc.

In reflecting on crime, it is important to recognize and accept the emotional responses which crime breeds. Anger, fear, outrage, are all predictable, "natural" reactions to crime. It would be foolish to attempt to ignore or repress such feelings. As Christians, our task is to come to grips with such feelings, and to overcome them. The challenge presented by Jesus in his teaching is to take the "long view" of life, to see beyond the immediate situation to something more permanent. Ultimately, what Jesus challenges us to do is develop a particular outlook on life, and its situations—one of love. Thus, in confronting crime, while certain emotional backlash is to be expected, he calls us to liberate ourselves from the emotions of the moment, and to respond in a way consistent with our Christian belief.

This does not mean Christians must be naive; that they must ignore the threat to the community which crime represents. What it does mean is that it is wrong to seek revenge; that it is wrong to hurt the offender more than is necessary for the community's protection; that it is wrong to dehumanize offenders; that it is wrong to refuse them any chance for reconciliation with the community; and that it is wrong to selectively perceive only the injustices wrought by offenders, while ignoring the injustices committed against them.

In short, our first task is to clarify our thinking on the subject of crime, and to begin the development of more Christian attitudes on crime control and the treatment of offenders. While Christians can do this individually, it would be all the more effective if churches were to spend a Sunday reflecting on crime; if bishops were to write to their congregations and guide their reflections; or if clergymen were to designate a day to preach on the subject of criminal justice. While attitudinal change is one of the more elusive goals which Christians can pursue, it is perhaps the most crucial of all.

Theological Change

If Christians are eventually to change their attitudes on crime and punishment, this necessarily involves a change in the ways in which Christian theologians address such subjects as law, justice, governmental authority, the nature of punishment, etc. As discussed earlier, frequently Christian theology has failed to take notice of the many inhumanities which permeate our system of criminal justice, and has simplistically assumed that American institutions are dedicated to the pursuit of Christian ideals. Rather than serve as a challenge to these institutions, Christian theology has usually served as a source of support. Clearly, however, we are confronted with a post-Christian Age, and a Christian theology which fails to recognize the incompatibility of American penal ideology with Christian faith is a theology of little service to the church. The following are suggested as parameters for building a more viable Christian "theology of criminal justice".

First, we should stop trying to glorify the institutions of government, and trying to consecrate them to the service of Christian ideals. While the institutions of American criminal law are largely derived from Christian thought and practice, and while Judeo-Christian ideals are frequently invoked in their defense, there is precious little that is Christian about their philosophy or practices. While Christians rightfully should attempt to humanize these institutions, we are mistaken if we try to declare them Christian, or expect that they can serve Christian ideals. From a social perspective, some form of crime control will always be necessary, and in many ways prisons are an advance over earlier means of dealing with crime. Nonetheless, they are the products of fallen humanity, not divine inspiration, and the Church can only lose credibility by attempting to support or "baptize" such institutions.

This in turn requires us to discard many medieval assumptions about the alliance of Church and state, and about the ways in which God works his saving grace in the world. Whatever means he chooses, history should have taught us that it is not through social and political institutions that God most frequently works. To assume therefore that the secular works of law and government mirror God's will or ways, as was frequently assumed in medieval times, is an error.

Second, we should be more precise about how we use terms that have both secular and religious meanings; terms such as law, justice, punishment, and even sin. It is understandable, because of their historical evolution, that there should be much confusion about the biblical or religious meanings of a concept as opposed to the secular and social meanings. However, the time has arrived for Christian writers to become more demanding of themselves and their colleagues in confronting social issues. Thus, when confronted by a statement such as "justice demands punishment", Christians might slowly become more aware that the "justice" to which a politician or columnist refers may well not be the same "justice" invoked by Jesus and the prophets before him, and that a Christian view of punishment is somewhat more sensitive to offenders than popular cries of "lock them up" may be.

Third, Christian writers need to develop a more critical attitude toward the state and the institutions of government. Many Christian theologians have begun to criticize the government, galvanized by issues such as the Viet Nam War, the world hunger crisis, and abortion. Not much of this criticism has filtered down to criminal justice. Probably this is because the theological concepts which buttress the criminal justice system are so complex, and have such a long history. Likewise, criminal justice is not quite so visible or sympathetic an issue as those others. Yet, traditional Christian teachings, which have simply not been re-evaluated, continue to lend support to our existing means of dealing with crime. The best remedy for this situation would be some truly prophetic criticism of governmental institutions as they are, as opposed to more abstract theorizing about what government can or should be.

Finally, in all of our "theologizing" and theorizing about social issues like crime, we should adopt a person-centered approach. In Rahner's terms, we should undertake "theological anthropology". While it might be fascinating to discuss law and punishment in the abstract, it is vital that we begin to discuss them as they concretely affect the lives of human beings. Discourses on the cleansing or medicinal purposes of punishment are simply irrelevant when Christians are faced with a dehumanizing system of criminal justice, such as exists today. Theories of justice are useless if those theories do nothing to prevent the infliction of needless suffering on thousands of people. For, every theory or idea ultimately has its impact on human lives, and it is with human life that Jesus, and therefore Christians, are concerned with more than any other subject. Jesus' personalistic ministry, in which he cared first for the needs of people, and only secondarily with abstract ideas, should be our guide. To the extent that Christian theology remains centered in the abstract, and fails to come to grips with the struggles of people, then it will be of little value to Christians who wish to bear witness in their lives.

Christian Action

Aside from the somewhat intangible steps of attitudinal and theological development, Christians can directly involve themselves in humanizing the criminal justice system. First, they can inform themselves of the realities of the courts and prisons in their own city or town. A team of clergymen, laity and religious can begin reading to inform themselves of basic issues and problems. Then they can visit with prison administrators, with judges, prosecutors, police officials, and prisoners themselves, in order to gain first-hand knowledge and experience with the system. Don't be surprised to find that individuals in official capacities will be willing to meet and talk with you. At the same time, don't be hesitant to insist that they do. The institutions of the criminal justice system belong to the citizenry, and are supported by your taxes. You have a right to scrutinize them and seek answers to your questions.

Likewise, don't accept everything that you are told at face value. A prison warden might give a glowing description of a program which serves only five inmates at a time. A judge might be so intent upon justifying his decisions that he slants his presentation to you. A prisoner might be so embittered by his experiences that he purposefully misleads you, or might be so intimidated that he merely mouths the official prison line about actual conditions. On the other hand, be sympathetic to the problems which are brought to your attention, whether from the standpoint of officials or offenders. If you are perceived as unwilling to listen and to learn, your chance of touching the lives of others are minimal.

Second, Christians, either in self-appointed groups or through organized structures such as church groups, schools, or parishes, should invite criminal justice officials and ex-inmates alike to come visit them. Invite them to your services, invite them to your discussion groups, invite them to your social affairs.

Engage them in your own activities, so that you can influence their lives and be a source of support to them. Ask yourself how it is that you can convey to them some assistance rooted in faith. Perhaps you can give a trial judge a better understanding of the lives of the prisoners who come before him. Perhaps a guard can be persuaded to overcome his bitterness toward prisoners generally, and to treat them as individuals. Perhaps an ex-inmate can be convinced that there are more fruitful ways to spend the remainder of his life than in commuting between the street life and the prison. Perhaps, most importantly, you can bring both officials and offenders more in contact with the community, and more in contact with one another as human beings.

Finally, and most importantly, Christians should make their presence felt in the prisons themselves. This presence can be achieved indirectly, by lobbying with legislators and criminal justice officials to develop a more human criminal justice system. Options such as work-release, whereby prisoners work at a job in the community while serving a sentence, halfway houses, where prisoners live in the community under supervision, and small-group prisons have been tried with great success in many locations. Moreover, alternatives to incarceration, such as restitution, have also worked in various locations around the country. Christians who wish to familiarize themselves with such efforts can obtain a handbook from a Quaker group working for the abolition of prisons, and can then urge that such innovations be adopted in their community or state.[1]

More directly, Christians can go and serve in the prisons themselves. In recent years, the use of lay volunteers in prisons has been increasingly accepted, to the point where it is now commonplace. Virtually all large prison systems, and many county jails and court systems as well, have developed programs through which individual citizens can volunteer their help.

Many institutions allow lay volunteers to provide elemental counseling for prisoners, probationers, and parolees. Such counseling is usually supported with training and supervision by professionals, so that a lack of credentials on the part of volunteers is not critical. Moreover, since the most important aspect of counseling is the establishment of a genuine, caring relationship between two human beings, lay volunteers are frequently as effective as professionals, who can be saddled with large case loads, and jaded by their experiences. National clearinghouses with information about such programs have been established to direct you in your search.[2] There are existing programs to which you can write for information.[3] And, finally, in the event that there are no existing vehicles for involvement in your community, models have been developed which will guide you in getting involved.[4]

Christians who have specific talents can volunteer them at a nearby institution. Volunteers at prisons across the country have provided regular and remedial academic courses, vocational training, as well as recreational direction for prisons. Likewise, Christians can involve themselves in the religious program of the institution, provided that they do so with an attitude which treats inmates as people in themselves, and not just as converts-to-be. If the prison in your community does not have a volunteer office, then you should contact the warden or the chaplain at the prison.

Finally, Christians can involve themselves in assisting prisoners after their release. Church groups can establish centers for ex-convicts to stay in or visit. Likewise, churches can hire ex-offenders and urge their members to do so. And individual Christians can offer jobs to men upon release. Again, there are existing organizations to serve as resources or models.[5] Or, the warden or chaplain at the local prison should be able to provide you with referrals and suggestions.

Actual presence of Christians in prisons has multiple advantages. By definition it improves conditions at the prison, since they are providing needed service, and, since institutions which are routinely visited by the community cannot become snake-pits as easily as institutions which the community ignores. Christian presence is also the most effective means of touching the lives of those in prisons, both prisoners and staff. It makes Christian faith concrete, and gives it credibility. Both staff and inmates will recognize what you stand for if you remain true to your ideals, and this example will have far more impact than anything which occurs outside of the prison walls. Finally, actual involvement keeps us from becoming stale in faith, from preaching but never practicing what we believe.

There are dangers to Christian volunteerism. There is the problem of being co-opted by the system; of simply supporting a corrupt system by providing band-aid services without effecting any significant change. There is a danger of becoming moralistic, and of treating prisoners as targets for conversion; or the means whereby Christians relieve themselves of guilt feelings. Then, there is the danger of being perceived as a naive "do-gooder", who has little understanding of the perversions of criminal justice. These difficulties are no excuse for non-involvement, however. They are merely realistic appraisals of the obstacles involved in bringing a truly Christian presence to prisons.

Perhaps the greatest difficulty of all, however, is that those who undertake work in this field will find little support for their work, and probably not even the satisfaction of seeing the fruits of their labors. A ministry in criminal justice, whether by a minister or a lay person, is probably one of the most demanding apostolates which one could undertake. There is little acclaim, and little success, on either side of the prison walls. And yet, "Happy are those who work for peace among men: God will call them His sons!" (Matt: 5:9)

NOTES

Introduction

1. A number of denominations have issued statements on criminal justice in recent years. In 1970, the World Council of Churches held a Consultation on Penal Policies, with representatives from 14 countries, and issued a report criticizing penal practices. In America, the US Catholic Conference, the Lutheran Church in America, the Episcopal Church of America and probably others as well, have all issued statements critical of American criminal justice. A number of religious orders in the Roman church have made studies of the problem and issued recommendations. Finally, an Interreligious Task Force on Criminal Justice was formed in 1973, the purpose of which was to study the problem and make practical suggestions for reform. As a rule, however, these documents have been very cautious in criticism, and have failed to issue any prophetic calls for radical change. The strongest of these statements, entitled *A Call For Action* came from the Jesuit Conference on Criminal Justice in *1973*.

2. Jessica Mitford, *Kind and Usual Punishment* (New York: Alfred A. Knopf, 1973), p. 297.

3. Gustavo Gutierrez, *A Theology of Liberation* (New York: Orbis Books, 1973), p. 11.

4. David Tracy, *Blessed Rage for Order* (New York: The Seabury Press, 1975), p. 243.

5. Jurgen Moltmann, *Hope and Planning* (New York: Harper & Row, 1971), p. 101. Note: This is not intended to say that the claims of faith must be empirically

212

verifiable, or capable of scientific proof. Rather, it is a warning that a theology based on wishful thinking, ignorant of historical reality, is a meaningless theology.

6. Karl Rahner, "Theology and Anthropology", *The Word in History*, ed. by T. Patrick Burke (New York: Sheed & Ward, 1966), p. 10.

7. Ibid., p. 1.

8. Ibid., p. 3.

9. Dietrich Bonhoeffer, *Ethics*, ed. by Eberhard Bethge and trans. by Neville Smith (New York: MacMillan, 1968).

Chapter 1

1. Moltmann, op. cit., p. 56.

2. A.E. Harvey, "Custody and the Ministry to Prisoners", *Theology*, Vol. 78 (1975), p. 82.

3. For a brief description of the Apostolic Constitution, see *The New Catholic Encyclopedia*, (New York: McGraw Hill, 1967) Vol. I, p. 689.

4. "Apostolic Constitutions", *The Ante-Nicene Fathers*, ed. by Rev. Alexander Roberts and James Donaldson, Vol. VII (Buffalo, New York: The Christian Literature Co., 1886), Chapter XIV, p. 381.

5. Ibid.

6. Ibid., Chapter XV, p. 402.

7. Ibid., Chapter XLVI, p. 417.

8. Raymond Salielles, *The Individualization of Punishment* (Boston: Little, Brown, and Co., 1913) pp. 30-34.

9. Ibid., p. 37.

10. Ibid., p. 35.

11. Charles Cochrane, *Christianity and Classical Culture*, (New York: Oxford Universal Press, 1944), for a description of Constantine's goals with respect to Christianity.

12. Herbert Workman, "Constantine", *Encyclopedia of Religion and Ethics*, ed. by James Hastings (New York: Charles Scribner's Sons, 1955), Vol. IV, p. 80.

13. Cochrane, op. cit., p. 203.

14. Massey H. Shephard, "Before and After

Constantine", *The Impact of the Church Upon Its Culture*, ed. by Jerald Brauer (Chicago: University of Chicago Press, 1968), p. 26.

15. *Codex Theodosius*, XVI. I. 2.

16. Cochrane, op. cit., p. 336.

17. Gerd Tellenbach, *Church, State and Christian Society at the Time of the Investiture Contest*, trans. by R.F. Bennett (New York: Harper & Row, 1959, 1970), p. 30.

18. Ambrose, *Duties of the Clergy*—Book II, in *Nicene and Post-Nicene Fathers*, ed. by Phillip Schaff and Jenry Wace (Buffalo, New York: The Christian Literature Co., 1896), Vol. X, p. 59, Chap. XXI, no, 102.

19. Ibid.

20. Ibid., p. 136, Chap. XXVIII.

21. Ibid., *The Confessions and Letters of St. Augustine*, Vol. I, Letter CXXXIII, to Marcellinus (412 A.D.), pp. 470-471.

22. *Constitutiones Sermondianae* (333 A.D.) i. 27. I 318, See Cochrane, op. cit., p. 204.

23. R.W. Southern, *Western Society and the Church in the Middle Ages* (Maryland: Penguin Books, 1970), p. 16.

24. Norman Zacour, *An Introduction to Medieval Institutions* (New York: St. Martin's Press, 1969), p. 139.

25. Adapted from University of Pennsylvania *Translations and Reprints* by Zacour, Vol. VI, no. 4, p. 11.

26. As far as this author knows, Mabillon's work on prisons, entitled *Reflections on the Prisons of the Monastic Orders*, has not been translated into English. However, part of his work has been reproduced by Thorsten Sellin, in his article "Dom Jean Mabillon—A Prison Reformer of the 17th Century", *Journal of Criminal Law and Criminology*, Vol. XVII, pp. 581-602. The passages referred to in this text are from pp. 584-585.

27. Ibid., pp. 586-587.

28. Ibid., pp. 599-600.

29. H.D. Hazeltine, (University of Cambridge), "Canon Law", *Encyclopedia of the Social Sciences*, ed. by Edwin R.A. Seligman, Vol. III (New York: MacMillan Co., 1930), p. 182.

30. William L. Clark and William L. Marshall, *A Treatise on the Law of Crimes,* 6th Edition, (Chicago: Callaghan, 1958), pp. 11-12.

31. John Kaplan, Criminal Justice—*Introductory Cases and Materials* (Mineola, New York: Foundation Press, 1973), pp. 31-32.

This definition of crime, as involving both act and intent, was later adopted wholesale by civil courts, and has found its way into modern usage. Today, both American and English common law definitions of crime describe "actus reus" and "mens rea" as necessary components for there to be a crime in the legal sense. It is because of the doctrine of "mens rea" that modern criminal courts frequently entertain testimony on issues of motivation, intention, and sanity when making decisions about criminal liability. Today, if it can be shown that a defendent lacked criminal intention, then the accused can escape punishment.

32. Hazeltine, op. cit., p. 182.

33. A.S. Turberville, *Medieval Heretics and the Inquisition* (London: Archon Books, 1964), Chap. V, pp. 206-228, discusses penalties for heresy. As Tuberville notes, scholars are unanimous in their opinion that Church pleas for mercy were usually "pro forma".

34. Tellenbach, op. cit., p. 24.

35. Paul E. Sigmund, *Natural Law in Political Thought*, (Cambridge, Mass.: Winthrop Publishers, 1971), Chap. 3 discusses medieval conceptions of natural law.

36. Bonaventure, *Commentary on Ecclesiastes* generally. Also Bede Jarnette, O.P., *Social Theories of the Middle Ages 1200-1500* (Maryland: The Newman Book Shop, 1942). See chapter on law.

37. Hazeltine, op. cit., p. 184.

38. Nicholas Kittrie, *The Right To Be Different, Deviance and Enforced Therapy* (Baltimore, Maryland: Penguin Books, 1973) pp. 13-14.

39. Ernst Troeltsch, *The Social Teaching of the Christian Churches*, trans. by Olive Wyon (New York: MacMillan Co., 1931) p. 549. Luther's stand on punishment is ironic in light of his highly critical attitude toward the state. Luther criticized the Roman Church for "historicizing" Christianity and sanctifying political power.

He maintained a clear distinction between spiritual and political authority. Yet, in developing his thought on how it is that God is present in the world, he ultimately sanctioned the use of naked force by the state in maintaining order; "The princes of this world are gods, the common people are Satan."

40. Ibid., p. 615.

41. See Georg Lee Haskins, *Law and Authority in Early Massachusetts* (New York: The MacMillan Co., 1960), for an interesting case study of the application of Calvin's ideas to American colonization.

42. Thomas Aquinas, *Summa Theologica* (many translations), 2,2, gv. xi, art. 3.

43. Cf. Thomas Merton's *Contemplation in a World of Action* (Garden City, New York: Image Books—Doubleday & Co., 1973), p. 163. On medieval conceptions of the world—"This view too is static rather than dynamic, hierarchic, layer upon layer, rather than on-going and self-creating, the fulfillment of a predetermined intellectual plan rather than the creative project of a free self-building love."

44. Peter Muller-Goldkuhle, "Developments in Eschatological Thought", *The Problem of Eschatology*, ed. by Edward Schillcbeeckx and Boniface Willems (New York: Paulist Press, 1969), p. 30 f.

45. "Apostolic Constitutions", *Ante-Nicene Fathers*, op. cit., Chap. XLIII, p. 416.

46. See generally, Thomas A. Shannon, *Render Unto God—A Theology of Selective Obedience* (New York: Paulist Press, 1974).

47. Sellin, op. cit., p. 583.

48. This would fall under the realm of "apologetic" theology, which according to Paul Tillich seeks to answer the perennial question: "Can the Christian message be adapted to the modern mind (and situation) without losing its essential and unique character?"

Chapter 2

1. Richard Quinney, *The Social Reality of Crime* (Boston: Little, Brown and Co., 1970), p. 64.

2. David J. Rothman, *The Discovery of the Asylum,*

Social Order and Disorder in the New Republic (Boston: Little, Brown and Co., 1971), see chapter 1, generally.

3. Noah Hobart, *Excessive Wickedness, the Way to an Untimely Death* (New London, Co., 1786), p. 9, 13. Cited by Rothman.

4. Auguste Jorns, *The Quakers as Pioneers in Social Work*, trans. by Thomas Brown (New York: The MacMillan Co., 1931), p. 187.

5. Ibid., p. 187.

6. J. Bellers, "Some Reasons Against Putting Felons to Death", (1699) p. 17 ff. Quoted by Jorns, op. cit., p. 170.

7. Ibid.

8. See generally, Lawrence M. Friedman, *A History of American Law* (New York: Simon & Schuster, 1973). Also see Gerhard O.W. Mueller, *Crime, Law and the Scholars* (Seattle: University of Washington Press, 1969), Chaps. 1-7.

9. Blake McKelvey, *American Prisons—A Study in American Social History Prior to 1915* (Chicago: The University of Chicago Press, 1936), p. 5.

10. Frederick F. Power, Jr., *The Role of the Prison Chaplain—An Analysis of the Prison Ministry in Philadelphia from 1682 to 1970*, Unpublished Master's Thesis, Philadelphia Divinity School, May, 1971, Chap. VII.

11. O.A. Pendleton, "Prison Reform and the Evangelical Churches", *Prison Journal*, Vol. XXVII, No. 2 (1948), p. 386.

12. Powers, op. cit., p. 47.

13. *Report of the Morals Instructor of the Eastern State Penitentiary*, 1853.

14. Rothman, op. cit., p. 82.

15. John L. Gillin, *Criminology and Penology* (New York: D. Appleton-Century, 1945, 3rd edition), p. 377.

16. Harry Elmer Barnes, *The Evolution of Penology in Pennsylvania* (Indianapolis: The Bobbs-Merrill Co., 1927), p. 129.

17. *First and Second Annual Reports of the Inspectors of the Eastern State Penitentiary*, 1829-30, 1830-31, p. 7 f.

18. *Orlando Lewis, The Development of American*

Prison Customs, 1776–1845 (Montclair, New Jersey: Patterson-Smith, 1967) p. 78.

19. Quoted by Mitford, op. cit., p. 32.

20. Lewis, op. cit., p. 87.

21. Ibid., p. 100.

22. Lewis, op. cit., p. 101.

23. "Annual Report of Auburn Prison", *New York Assembly Documents*, 1840 I. No. 18, pp. 13-14.

24. Robert M. Senkewicz, "Early American Innocence and the 'Modern' Prison", *America* (April 24, 1976), p. 355.

25. Sellin, op. cit., p. 587. See footnote 26, chapter one, above.

26. Ibid.

27. Senkewicz, op. cit., p. 355.

28. Mitford, op. cit., p. 33.

29. Ibid.

30. Zebulon Brockway, *Fifty Years of Prison Service* (New York: Charities Publication Committee, 1912), p. 419.

31. *Ruffin v. The Commonwealth of Virginia*, United States Supreme Court, 1871.

32. Friedman, op. cit., p. 521.

33. Donald R. Cressey, "Adult Felons in Prison", *Prisoners in America*, Lloyd Ohlin, editor (Englewood Cliffs, New Jersey: Prentice-Hall 1973) p. 123.

34. Harry Barnes and Negley Teeters, *New Horizons In Criminology* (Englewood Cliffs, New Jersey: Prentice-Hall, 3rd edition, 1959), p. 339.

35. Quoted by Mitford, op. cit., p. 33.

36. Francis Bergan, "The Sentencing Power in Criminal Cases", *13 Albany Law Review* (1949), p. 3.

37. Cressey, op. cit., p. 125.

38. Ramsey Clark, *Crime in America* (New York: Simon & Schuster, 1970), p. 59.

39. Karl Menninger, *The Crime of Punishment* (New York: Viking Press, 1969), p. 19.

40. Kittrie, op. cit., p. 30.

41. Today most jurisdictions retain some form of indeterminate sentence, which is intended to "motivate"

prisoners not to cause trouble, and to participate in treatment programs.

42. Revealed by David A. Ward, "Evaluative Research for Corrections", *Prisoners in America*, ed. by Lloyd Ohlin, The American Assembly (Englewood Cliffs, New Jersey: Prentice-Hall Inc., 1973), p. 190.

43. Thomas Szasz, *Ideology and Insanity—Essays on the Psychiatric Dehumanization of Man* (Garden City, New York: Doubleday & Co., Inc., 1970), p. 36.

44. Mitford, op. cit., p. 97.

45. Kittrie, op. cit., p. 31.

46. Szasz, op. cit., p. 5.

47. Harvey Powelson and Richard Bendix, "Psychiatry in Prison", *Psychiatry*, Vol. XIV (1951).

48. *Deterrent Effects of Criminal Sanctions, Progress Report of the Assembly Committee on Criminal Procedure* (Sacramento, California, May, 1968).

49. John Irwin, *The Felon* (Englewood Cliffs, New Jersey: Prentice—Hall, 1970), p. 57.

50. Quoted by Mitford, op. cit., p. 120.

51. See Mitford, op. cit., "Clockwork Orange", chap. 8, for more details.

52. Examples of such studies would be: C.V. Dunn, "The Church and Crime in the United States", *The Annals*, Vol. 117 (May, 1926), pp. 200-228; Franklin Steiner, *Religion and Roguery* (New York: The Truth Seeker, 1924); P.R. Hightower, *Biblical Information in Relation to Character and Conduct* (Iowa City: University of Iowa Press, 1930).

53. Barnes and Teeters, op. cit., p. 494.

54. Barnes and Teeters, op. cit., p. 495.

55. *Chaplains Manual* (Philadelphia Department of Prisons), no imprint, p. 2.

56. *Manual of Standards*, American Correctional Association (Washington, D.C., 1959), p. 472.

57. Ronald Goldfarb, *Jails—The Ultimate Ghetto* (New York: Anchor Press/Doubleday & Co., Inc., 1975), p. 13.

58. *Network Quarterly*, Vol. III, no. 2 (Summer, 1975).

59. Goldfarb, op. cit., p. 14.

60. Elizabeth Flynn, "Jails and Criminal Justice", *Prisoners in America*, ed. by Lloyd Ohlin, The American Assembly (Englewood Cliffs, New Jersey: Prentice—Hall, 1973), p. 55.

61. Goldfarb, op. cit., p. 2.

62. Leonard Downie, Jr., *Justice Denied, the Case for the Reform of Courts* (Baltimore, Maryland: Penguin Books, 1971), see chap. 3.

63. Flynn, op. cit., p. 57.

64. Goldfarb, op. cit., p. 33.

65. President's Crime Commission Task Force Report on the Courts (US Government Printing Office, 1967), p. 18.

66. Flynn, op. cit., p. 64.

67. Mitford, op. cit., p. 276.

68. Donald Taft, *Criminology* (New York: MacMillan, 3rd edition, 1956), p. 134.

69. James Steele and Donald Bartlett, "Justice in Philadelphia", *The New Republic* (May, 1973), p. 20.

70. The Challenge of Crime in a Free Society (US Government Printing Office, Washington, D.C., Feb., 1967), p. 172.

71. Clark, op. cit., p. 219.

72. Cressey, op. cit., pp. 125, 129.

73. Ibid., p. 124.

74. Paul W. Keve, *Prison Life and Human Worth* (Minneapolis: University of Minnesota Press, 1975), p. 13.

75. "Struggle for Justice: A Report on Crime & Punishment in America", American Friends Service Committee (New York: Hill & Wang, 1971), p. 96.

76. Keve, op. cit., p. 52.

77. Ibid., p. 16.

78. Report on Corrections (US Government Printing Office, Washington, D.C., 1973), p. 1.

Chapter 3

1. Quinney, op. cit., p. 286.

2. Neil Shover, "Criminal Behavior As Theoretical Praxis", *Issues in Criminology*, Vol. 10, no. 1 (Spring, 1975), pp. 95-105.

3. Milton E. Burglass, *The Thresholds Program: A Community Based Intervention in Correctional Therapeutics* (Cambridge, Mass.: Correctional Solutions, Inc., 1972), p. 20.

4. Barnes and Teeters, op. cit., p. 7.

5. Barnes and Teeters, op. cit., p. 51.

6. Bruce Jackson, *In the Life: Versions of the Criminal Experience* (Times Mirror, New York: New American Library, 1974), p. 3.

7. Burglass, op. cit., p. 24.

8. According to Barnes and Teeters, "studies made by clinical psychologists of prison populations (inmates) demonstrate that those behind bars compare favorably with the general population in intelligence, op. cit., p. 7. For an example of such a study see G.R. Pierson and R.F. Kelley, "HSPQ norms on a statewide prison population", Journal of Psychology, Vol. 56, (1963), pp. 185-192.

9. The avalanche of writing from American prisons since the mid-1960's should be enough to dispel popular myths about inmate's lack of mental ability. e.g. Eldridge Cleaver's *Soul on Ice* (New York: McGraw-Hill, 1967). George Jackson, *Soledad Brother: The Prison Letters of George Jackson* (New York: Coward-McCann, 1970), etc.

10. I am indebted to Ed Denion, S.J., a former prison chaplain, for this particular insight.

11. Jackson, op. cit., p. 8.

12. Edwin H. Sutherland, *The Professional Thief* (Chicago: University of Chicago Press, 1937).

13. Irwin, op. cit., p. 24. Others who have recognized this pattern include Donald Gibbons, *Society, Crime and Criminal Careers* (Englewood Cliffs, New Jersey: Prentice-Hall, 1968); and Julian Roebuck, "The Jack-of-all-Trades Offender", *Crime and Delinquency,* (April, 1962).

14. Cited by Barry Krisberg, "Gang Youth and Hustling: The Psychology of Survival", *Issues in Criminology*, Vol. 9, no. 1 (Spring, 1974), p. 122.

15. Burglass, op. cit., p. 26.

16. David Matza, *Delinquency and Drift* (New York: John Wiley and Sons, Inc., 1964), p. 87.

17. Ibid., p. 88.

18. Julian Roebuck, "The Short 'Con Man' ", *Crime and Delinquency*, (July, 1964), pp. 241, 243.

19. Edmond Cahn, *The Sense of Injustice* (Bloomington, Indiana: Indiana University Press, 1964 edition).

20. Irwin, op. cit., p. 51.

21. Grahm Sykes, *Crime and Society* (New York: Random House, 2nd edition, 1967), p. 119.

22. Irwin, op. cit., p. 11.

23. Sykes, op. cit., *(Crime and Society)-*, p. 127.

24. Grahm Sykes, *The Society of Captives* (Princeton, New Jersey: Princeton University Press, 1958), pp. 66-67.

25. Lloyd McCorke and Richard Korn, *Annals of the American Academy of Political and Social Science*, Vol. 293 (1954), p. 88.

26. Matza, op. cit., p. 41.

27. Unpublished poem by a resident of the Pennsylvania State Correctional Institution at Graterford.

28. Keve, op. cit., p. 6.

29. Bill Larson, now Kansas Director of the 7th Step Foundation. Quoted by Bill D. Schul, *St. Anthony's Messenger*, Vol. 78 (February, 1971), p. 29.

30. Barnes and Teeters, op. cit., note that many chaplains have in fact become "institutionalized", p. 493.

31. Francis J. Miller, "The Inmate's Attitude Toward Religion and the Chaplain", *Proceedings* (The American Correctional Association, 1941), pp. 431-435.

32. Schul, op. cit., p. 28.

33. Ibid., p. 30.

Chapter 4

1. H.L.A. Hart, "Murder and the Principles of Punishment: England and the United States", 52 Northwestern L. Rev. (1957), pp. 446-447.

2. Karl Menninger, *The Crime of Punishment*, op. cit., p. 198.

3. John Sheehan, S.J., *The Threshing Floor, An Interpretation of the Old Testament* (New York: Paulist Press, 1972), p. 191.

4. Roland de Vaux, *Ancient Israel* (New York: McGraw-Hill Book Co., Inc., 1961), p. 149.

5. Ibid., p. 158.

6. Emil Brunner, *Justice and the Social Order* (New York: Harper and Row, 1945), p. 118.

7. Ibid., p. 120.

8. Sheehan, op. cit., p. 144.

9. Pope Pius XII, "Crime and Punishment", *Contemporary Punishment: Views, Explanations and Justifications*, ed. by Rudolph Gerber and Patrick McAnany (Notre Dame, Indiana: University of Notre Dame Press, 1972) pp. 59-72.

10. Lincoln T. Bouscaren, S.J. and Adam C. Ellis, S.J., *Canon Law, A Text and Commentary* (Milwaukee, Wisconsin: The Bruce Publishing Co., 1946), p. 808.

11. Pius XII, op. cit., p. 63.

12. Ibid., p. 61.

13. Ibid., p. 65.

14. Ibid.

15. The following comparison was suggested by John Shea, *What a Modern Catholic Believes About Heaven and Hell* (Chicago: The Thomas More Press, 1972), p. 48.

16. A. Renan, *History of the People of Israel* (1894), cited by Boaz Cohen, *Law and Tradition in Judaism* (New York: Ktav Publishing House, Inc., 1969), pp. 191-192.

17. Cohen, op. cit., p. 191.

18. Toby Jackson "Is Punishment Necessary", *Contemporary Punishment: Views, Explanations and Justifications*, op. cit., p. 225.

19. Karl Menninger, *The Crime of Punishment*, op. cit., see chap. 3.

20. While C.S. Lewis is frequently cited as advocating retribution, he did so reluctantly, because he saw other justifications for punishment as even more dangerous for criminals. Cf. C.S. Lewis, "The Humanitarian Theory of Punishment", *Contemporary Punishment*, op. cit., pp. 194-199.

21. Emil Brunner, *Justice and the Social Order*, op. cit., p. 223.

22. Boaz Cohen, *Law and Tradition in Judaism*, op. cit., p. 183.

23. See John H. Yoder, *The Politics of Jesus* (Michigan:

223

Williams B. Eerdmans Publishing Co., 1972), for a good critique of a "personalistic" interpretation of the Gospel.

24. Leslie Dewert, *The Future of Belief* (New York: Herder and Herder, 1966), p. 29.

25. Brian Barry, *Political Argument* (London: Routledge and Kegan Paul, 1965), p. 112.

26. Norval Morris, "Impediments to Penal Reform", 33 University of Chicago L. Rev. (1966) p. 63.

27. Franklin Zimring and Gordon Hawkins, *Deterrence* (Chicago: University of Chicago Press, 1973) p. 19.

28. Keve, op. cit., p. 186.

29. National Advisory Commission on Criminal Justice Standards and Goals, Report on Corrections, Law Enforcement Assistance Agency (1973).

30. Kant's argument, in his *Philosophy of Law*, was that it is immoral to ever treat people as means to an end.

31. Jacques Maritain, *The Rights of Man and Natural Law*, trans. by Doris C. Anson (New York: Charles Scribner's Sons, 1943), p. 2.

32. Ibid., p. 3.

33. Ibid., p. 4.

34. Bernard Haring, *Ethics of Manipulation, Issues in Medicine, Behavior Control and Genetics* (New York: The Seabury Press, 1975), p. 52.

35. See Victor Frankl, *Man's Search for Meaning* (New York: Pocket Books, Simon and Schuster, 1963).

36. Mike Middleton, a former prisoner, quoted by Philip Zimbardo, "A Pirandellian Prison", *New York Times Magazine* (April 8, 1973), p. 47.

37. Karl Barth, *Against the Stream: Shorter Post-War Writings 1946-1952)* (New York: Philosophical Library, 1954), p. 36.

38. Hardy Goransson, "Human Dignity in the Execution of Punishment", *Studies in Penology*, ed. by Manuel Lopez Key and Charles Germain (The Hague: Martinus Mijhoff, 1964), p. 108.

39. Ibid.

40. Ibid., p. 109.

41. Immanuel Kant, *Philosophy of Law*, many translations.

42. Reinhold Niebuhr, *Nature and Destiny of Man*, vol.

1 Human Nature (New York: Charles Scribner's Sons, 1957), p. 57.

43. Jacques Maritain, *The Rights of Man and Natural Law*, op. cit., p. 7.

44. Ibid., p. 8.

45. Ibid., p. 9.

46. This position is by no means confined to Catholic theology. Emil Brunner, the great Protestant writer, advanced a similar model of the common good in his *Justice and the Social Order*, op. cit., p. 43. "Man does not derive his *dignity* from service to the whole. His dignity as a person is anterior to fellowship because every individual is called by God Himself and is personally responsible to Him. The corporate community does not stand above the individual, making him a dependent, a subordinate part of a higher whole, but fellowship is only personal when it is a community of independent, responsible persons."

47. Victor Frankl, *The Doctor and the Soul* (New York: Vintage Books, A Division of Random House, 1973), p. xix.

48. Cited by Schul, *St. Anthony's Messenger*, op. cit., p. 28.

49. Bernard Haring, *Ethics of Manipulation*, op. cit., p. 50.

50. Ibid., p. 51.

51. Victor Frankl, *The Doctor and the Soul*, op. cit., p. xxi.

52. Social psychologists have found direct links between individuals' images of themselves and their behavior. See Eliott Aronson, *The Social Animal* (New York: Viking Press, 1972).

53. In 1970, during the Nixon administration, the President's physician Arnold Hutschnecker proposed "massive psychological testing of six to eight-year old children to determine which were criminally inclined, and the establishment of special camps to house those found to have violent tendencies." Coincidentally, this was Dr. Hutschnecker's alternative plan to slum reconstruction. Mitford, *Kind and Usual Punishment*, op. cit., p. 56.

54. Roosevelt Murray spent sixteen years in Maryland "treatment" centers and prisons after being committed under an indeterminate sentence for joyriding in a stolen auto. After

225

his court-ordered release, he described the Patuxent treatment facility as a place "where men are destroyed. They try to break you down inch by inch and then reassemble you in their image."

55. Thomas Szasz, *Ideology and Insanity*, op. cit., See especially chapters 4, 5 and 7.

56. Founded by William Glasser, *Reality Therapy: A New Approach to Psychiatry* (New York: Harper and Row, 1965).

Chapter 5

1. The term "Church" here is used in the broad sense of the word, referring to all those who embrace Christianity, without regard to denomination. While there are obvious differences among the various denominations, especially concerning specific beliefs, these differences do not have a marked affect on the way in which the Christian Churches function as a cultural force. And while there are specific exceptions to the statements made in this chapter about the Church, in general the criticisms advanced here are applicable on a wide scale.

2. While this metaphor was first suggested by the Roman Church during Vatican II, it also has value as a description for the Christian Church in general. Cf. "Lumen Gentium", The Dogmatic Constitution on the Church.

3. Michael Novak, "The Absolute Future", *New Theology no. 5*, ed. by Martin E. Marty and Dean G. Peerman (New York: The MacMillan Co., 1968), p. 205.

4. Marie Augusta Neal, S.N.D., "Civil Religion, Theology and Politics in America", *America in Theological Perspective*, ed. by Thomas M. McFadden (New York: The Seabury Press, 1976), p. 106.

5. Ibid., p. 107.

6. H. Richard Niebuhr, *Christ and Culture* (New York: Harper and Row, 1951), p. 83.

7. Bishop John Wright, *The Christian and the Law* (Notre Dame, Indiana: Fides Publishers, Inc., 1962), pp. 14, 21.

8. Christopher Dawson, *Religion and Culture* Gifford Lectures (New York: Meridian Books, Inc., 1958), p. 206.

9. Neal, *America in Theological Perspective,* op. cit., p. 110.

10. Lutheran Church in America, Social Statements, *In Pursuit of Justice and Dignity: Society, the Offender and Systems of Correction* (New York: Board of Social Ministry, Lutheran Church of America, 1972), p. 1.

11. The United States Catholic Conference, a formal statement, *The Reform of Correctional Institutions in the 1970's* (Washington, D.C.: The United States Catholic Conference, 1973), p. 5.

12. William Stringfellow, *An Ethic for Christians and Other Aliens in a Strangeland* (Waco, Texas: Word Books, Publisher, 1973), p. 21.

13. Frederick Herzog, "Whatever Happened to Theology", *Christianity and Crisis* (May 12, 1975), p. 116.

14. Reinhold Niebuhr, *Faith and Politics* (New York: George Braziller, 1968), p. 90.

15. See John H. Yoder, *The Politics of Jesus* (Grand Rapids, Michigan: William B. Eerdmans Publishing Co., 1972) or John L. McKenzie, *Light on the Epistles* (Chicago: The Thomas More Press, 1975), chap. 6.

16. See Tom Wicker, *A Time To Die* (New York: Quadrangle/The New York Times Book Co., 1975) for a brilliant and moving description of the Attica tragedy.

17. Wolfhart Pannenberg, "Toward a Theology of Law", *American Theological Review* vol. 55 (4) (1973), p. 397.

18. Jacques Ellul, *False Presence of the Kingdom* (New York: The Seabury Press, 1963).

19. Ibid., p. 16.

20. Cf. Pannenberg, op. cit., for a description of these efforts.

21. Gustavo Gutierrez, *A Theology of Liberation*, op. cit., p. 11.

22. Tom E. Driver, "Whatever Happened to Theology", *Christianity and Crisis*, op. cit., p. 118.

Chapter 6

1. Reinhold Niebuhr, *Faith and Politics*, op. cit., p. 131.

2. Hugo W. Thompson, *Love–Justice* (North Quincy,

Mass.: The Christopher Publishing House, 1970), p. 27.

3. Bernard Haring, *A Theology of Protest* (New York: Farrar, Straus and Giroux, 1970), p. 11. Also see Haring's "The Normative Value of the Sermon on the Mount", *Catholic Biblical Quarterly*, vol. XXIX (1967), pp. 375-385.

4. This approach is obviously inspired by recent attempts in Christian theology to consider the problem of "eschatology"—the final things—in terms of the gradual coming of the Kingdom inaugurated by Jesus. See Schillebeeckx, *The Problem of Eschatology*, op. cit., and *New Theology no. 5*, op. cit.

5. Gabriel Marcel, *Man Against Mass Society* (Chicago: Henry Regnery Co., 1952), p. 157.

6. Bernard Haring, *A Theology of Protest*, op. cit., p. 61.

7. Emil Brunner, *Justice and the Social Order*, op. cit., p. 16.

8. Ibid., pp. 19-20.

9. George Jackson, *Soledad Brother–The Prison Letters of George Jackson*, op. cit., p. 37.

10. A.E. Harvey, "Custody and the Ministry to Prisoners", *Theology*, op. cit., p. 88.

11. Patrick Kerans, *Sinful Social Structures* (New York: Paulist Press, 1974), p. 44.

Chapter 7

1. Raymond Saleilles, *The Individualization of Punishment*, op. cit., p. 65.

2. Ibid., p. 66.

3. Ibid., p. 86.

4. Gregory Baum, "The Grace To Be Well", *Holiness and Mental Health*, ed. by Alfred Joyce (New York: Paulist Press, 1972), pp. 127-128.

5. Ibid., p. 128.

6. Ibid., p. 129.

7. Ibid., p. 132.

8. John Swomley, Jr., *Liberation Ethics* (New York: The Macmillan Company, 1972), p. 44.

9. Patrick Kerans, *Sinful Social Structures*, op. cit.

10. See *New York Times Magazine* (April 8, 1973), p. 38 for a good description of the experiment.

11. Bruce Jackson, *In the Life*, op. cit., p. 26.

12. Oscar Wilde, "The Ballad of Reading Gaol".

13. Robert K. Merton, *Social Theory and Social Structure* (Glencoe, Illinois: Free Press, 1957), pp. 145-146.

14. A.E. Harvey, *Theology*, op. cit., p. 89.

15. Paul Tillich, *Systematic Theology*, vol. 2 (Chicago: University of Chicago Press, 1954), p. 59.

Chapter 8

1. This was the stand taken by Will D. Campbell and James Y. Holloway in their book ". . . *and the criminals with him* . . .", (New York: Paulist Press, 1973), pp. 140-151.

2. Paul Tillich, *The Eternal Now* (New York: Charles Scribner's Sons), p. 114.

3. William Stringfellow, *An Ethic for Christians and Other Aliens in a Strangeland*, op. cit., p. 31.

4. Paul Tillich, *The Eternal Now*, op. cit., pp. 115-116.

5. Carlo Carretto, *Letters from the Desert* (Maryknoll, New York: Orbis Books, 1976), p. 31.

6. Again it is important to emphasize that this does not constitute the Christian prison ministry everywhere.

7. Paul Tillich, *The Eternal Now*, op. cit., pp. 117-118.

8. For this insight I am again indebted to A.E. Harvey, *Theology*, op. cit., p. 87.

9. Martin Luther King, Jr., *Where Do We Go From Here: Chaos or Community?* (Boston: Beacon Press, 1967).

10. William Stringfellow, *Ethic* . . ., op. cit.

11. Jean Danielou, *Prayer as a Political Problem* (New York: Sheed and Ward, 1967), p. 7.

Chapter 9

1. Write to PREAP, 3049 E. Henessee St., Syracuse, New York, 13224. Ask for their handbook on the abolition of prisons, which costs approximately five dollars. It is filled with data on prisons, but more importantly it describes viable alternatives in detail.

2. Two fine sources of information on existing programs in criminal justice are:

The National Information Center
on Volunteerism
P.O. Box 4179
Boulder, Colorado 80302

"Volunteers in Probation"
200 Washington Square Plaza
Royal Oak, Michigan

3. Among the more successful programs are:
Amicus, Inc.
1009 Nicollet South
Minneapolis, Minnesota 55403

The Fortune Society
29 E. 22nd Street
New York, N.Y. 10010

The Thresholds Program
Correctional Solutions, Inc.
22 Ellsworth Avenue
Cambridge, Ma. 02139

4. Write to the Office of Health & Welfare, United Presbyterian Church, 475 Riverside Drive, Rm. 1244, New York, N.Y. 10027, and ask for their models for "connecting" with prisons.

5. For employment program models, write:
Rev. Dick Simmons
"Job Therapy, Inc."
150 John Street
Seattle, Washington 98109

The Prison Apostolate
Catholic Charities of the Archdiocese of New York
1011 First Avenue
New York, N.Y. 10022
In addition, the National Alliance of Businessmen has

begun a nation-wide program aimed at finding employment for ex-offenders. For information, contact the local NAB office in your area.

SELECT BIBLIOGRAPHY

General Works on Criminal Justice

Kind and Usual Punishment, Jessica Mitford, (New York: Alfred A. Knopf, 1973) An exceptionally well-written, well-researched critique of American prisons and their operation.

Prison Life and Human Worth, Paul Keve, (Minneapolis: University of Minnesota Press, 1975) A sensitive look at the human cost of imprisonment, written by a professional in the field.

Jails—The Ultimate Ghetto, Ronald Goldfarb, (New York: Anchor Press/Doubleday & Co., 1975) The best available resource on local county jails, their conditions and operation.

Prisoners in America, Lloyd Ohlin, ed., The American Assembly, (Englewood Cliffs, N.J.: Prentice-Hall, Inc., 1973) An informative anthology containing sensitive articles on a number of subjects.

Justice Denied, Leonard Downie, Jr., (Baltimore: Penguin Books, 1972) Good overall discussion of the inadequacies of the court system.

Crime & Justice in America, L. Harold DeWolf, (New York: Harper & Row, Publishers, 1975) An attempt to give an ethical perspective on the issues of criminal justice, with suggestions for reform.

Works on Penal Ideology

Contemporary Punishment: Views, Explanations, and Jus-

tifications, Rudolph Gerber and Patrick McAnany, eds., (Notre Dame, Indiana: University of Notre Dame Press, 1972) Excellent anthology which provides a representative sampling of all major theories for punishment.

The Right To Be Different: Deviance and Enforced Therapy, Nicholas Kittrie, (Baltimore: Penguin Books, 1971) Best available review of treatment theory and its implications.

Works Related to Ministry to Prisoners

The Felon, John Irwin, (Englewood Cliffs, N.J.: Prentice-Hall Inc., 1970) Excellent description of the life histories, lifestyles, and worldviews of the different "varieties" of offender one finds in prison. Best introduction to prisoners for those unfamiliar with them.

Ministering to Prisoners and Their Families, George C. Kandle and Henry Cassler, (Englewood Cliffs, N.J.: Prentice-Hall, Inc., 1967) Provides some useful information on the role of ministry in prisons, and a lengthy case study which is quite instructive.

". . . and the criminals with him . . ." lk. 23:33, W. Campbell and James Holloway, eds., (New York: Paulist Press, 1973) An anthology of prisoners' writings, providing excellent insights on life in prison, and the issues raised by American prisons.

"Custody and the Ministry to Prisoners", *Theology,* Vol. 78 (1975) p. 82, A.E. Harvey. Best available article on the theological basis for a ministry to prisons.

"Pastoral Theology in Prisons", *Clergy Review*, 53:925, Dec. 1968, A. Cunningham. Contrasts ministry in prisons with other ministries, and points out the qualities needed to minister successfully in prison.

Theological Works with some Relation to Criminal Justice

A Theology of Liberation, Gustavo Gutierrez, (New York: Orbis Books, 1973) Seminal work providing a theological basis for Christian concern over social issues and justice.

Justice and the Social Order, Emil Brunner, (New York: Harper and Row, 1945) While Brunner was a retributivist, this book contains many worthwhile insights on the relationship between Christianity and social institutions.

A Theology of Protest, Bernard Haring, (New York: Farrar, Strauss, and Giroux, 1970) Provides many insights on the necessity of resistance to oppressive social institutions.

Faith and Politics, Reinhold Niebuhr, (New York: George Braziller, 1968) A collection of essays, all quite realistic, which discuss the operation of Christian faith in the political world.

The Person and the Common Good, Jacques Maritain, (Notre Dame, Indiana: University of Notre Dame Press, 1972) Despite the difficulties of the natural law theory, this book contains many worthwhile insights on the primacy of people over institutions.

Christ and Culture, H. Richard Niebuhr, (New York: Harper and Row, Publishers, 1951) Discusses the way in which different Christians relate to the society at large. Provides a useful framework for analysis of Christian involvement in the larger society.

"Toward a Theology of Law", *Anglican Theological Review*, Vol. 55(4), 395-420, (1973), Wolfhart Pannenberg. A somewhat scholarly article, criticizing both Catholic and Protestant conceptions of law, and providing some interesting suggestions for future explorations in this area.